Teach Like a Magician

Unlock the magic of teaching! With this fun and thorough guide, learn how to inspire and captivate your students with the help of eight powerful, research-backed strategies. This book empowers educators to create dynamic, supportive, and high-impact learning environments, especially in challenging settings.

Through the MAGICIAN framework and supporting classroom stories and reflection questions, you'll discover how to:

- **Motivate** students and ignite their intrinsic drive;
- Foster **Active Learning** with hands-on, interactive methods;
- Set clear, **Goal-Oriented Instruction** that focuses on achievable objectives;
- Cultivate **Imaginative Teaching** to inspire creativity and critical thinking;
- Nurture **Creativity and Curiosity**, sparking a lifelong love of learning;
- **Immerse** yourself in your students' world to create deep, meaningful connections;
- Use **Affirmation** to provide positive reinforcement that builds confidence;
- Foster **Natural Rapport** to develop authentic, trusting relationships.

Drawing on the captivating qualities of magicians, *Teach Like a Magician* encourages early childhood, elementary, and special education teachers to use charisma, surprise, and creativity to engage students. By integrating elements of storytelling, illusion, and excitement into your lessons, you'll keep students motivated and actively involved, making learning unforgettable.

Kevin Spencer is an award-winning performing artist and renowned academic. His work focuses on using magic to help individuals with autism, developmental disabilities, intellectual challenges, emotional disturbances, and trauma histories. Dr. Spencer holds a Ph.D. in Special Education, a Master's in Arts and Academic Interdisciplinary Education, and certifications in Autism Studies and Trauma Support. He currently serves as faculty at prestigious institutions, including Harvard Medical Teaching Hospital's *Pediatric Sedation Conference* and the University of Alabama at Birmingham.

Also Available from Routledge Eye On Education
www.routledge.com/k-12

A Lasting Impact in the Classroom and Beyond: Knowledge and Insight for Brave Teachers
Larry Strauss

Six Principles for Building a Truly Inclusive School: A Call to Action for K–12 Leaders
Toni R. Barton

Tactile Tools for Social Emotional Learning: Activities to Help Children Self-Regulate with SEL, PreK-5
Lori Reichel

Unpacking Privilege in the Elementary Classroom: A Guide to Race and Inequity for White Teachers
Jacquelynne Boivin, Kevin McGowan

How to Get All Teachers to Become Like the Best Teachers
Todd Whitaker

Teach Like a Magician
8 Effective Teaching Tricks to Inspire and Engage Your Students

Kevin Spencer

NEW YORK AND LONDON

Designed cover image: Getty Images

First published 2026
by Routledge
605 Third Avenue, New York, NY 10158

and by Routledge
4 Park Square, Milton Park, Abingdon, Oxon, OX14 4RN

Routledge is an imprint of the Taylor & Francis Group, an informa business

© 2026 Kevin Spencer

The right of Kevin Spencer to be identified as author of this work has been asserted in accordance with sections 77 and 78 of the Copyright, Designs and Patents Act 1988.

All rights reserved. No part of this book may be reprinted or reproduced or utilised in any form or by any electronic, mechanical, or other means, now known or hereafter invented, including photocopying and recording, or in any information storage or retrieval system, without permission in writing from the publishers.

For Product Safety Concerns and Information please contact our EU representative GPSR@taylorandfrancis.com. Taylor & Francis Verlag GmbH, Kaufingerstraße 24, 80331 München, Germany.

Trademark notice: Product or corporate names may be trademarks or registered trademarks, and are used only for identification and explanation without intent to infringe.

ISBN: 978-1-041-11423-9 (hbk)
ISBN: 978-1-041-11417-8 (pbk)
ISBN: 978-1-003-65991-4 (ebk)

DOI: 10.4324/9781003659914

Typeset in Palatino
by codeMantra

Dedication

To my wife, Cindy, my most profound inspiration—your belief in me and the work we do together echoes through every page.

To my mother and father, who never stopped believing in me—your unwavering support has been my foundation.

To the students who have taught me more about patience, presence, and possibility than any textbook ever could—this is for you.

To the teachers who show up with open hands and open hearts—may you always find the magic in the messy, the joy in the challenge, and the beauty in being truly present.

And to every reader who finds a piece of themselves within these chapters—may you feel seen, encouraged, and reminded that your story matters.

You are the spark. You are the magic.

Contents

Forward viii
Meet the Author x

Why Did I Write This Book? 1

Introducing *Teach Like a Magician:* Unveiling the
Enchanting Art of Education 5

1 M is for Motivation 9

2 A is for Active Learning 19

3 G is for Goal-Directed Instruction 36

4 I is for Imaginative Teaching 48

5 C is for Creativity and Curiosity 60

6 I is for Immersion 72

7 A is for Affirmation 84

8 N is for Natural Rapport 93

9 Hocus Focus and Hocus Focus Analytics 103

10 The Final Bow 116

Foreword

Kevin Spencer is a master at keeping secrets. After all, he has decades of experience in following the Magician's Oath in concealing methods of how an illusion works. However, he has chosen to deviate from his oath of secrecy to reveal techniques honed on the stage to capture and maintain the unwavering attention of his audience. To that end, *Teach Like a Magician* unlocks the mystery of the tools of the trade to enhance student learning. These techniques are valuable to both pre-service teachers and experienced educators who increasingly need to create learning environments that are as compelling as those developed by professional entertainers.

Throughout his successful career as an entertainer, Kevin mastered techniques to gain his audience's attention, cultivate their curiosity, and motivate their interest in the art of illusion. When he was called to the teaching profession, he drew upon these abilities to engage learners and share these techniques with educators quite frankly, because they work. Teaching is an interdisciplinary endeavor. Good teaching is not a single skill set. It is both an art and a science which come together to make learning magical.

Personally, I had little experience with magic tricks and never appreciated the art of illusions until I had a chance to work with Kevin. During a special education conference, he convinced me that a curriculum of magic tricks might be beneficial to students with disabilities. My work in special education included 10 years of classroom teaching students with multiple disabilities and subsequently 27 years of training teachers in special education methodologies with special emphasis on utilizing innovative technologies. My research examined the effects of harnessing video conferencing technologies for dissemination and collaboration among professionals who might not otherwise be able to work together and to connect students with disabilities to peers across the globe.

Kevin and I decided to employ project-based learning within the scholar-practitioner model to understand how a virtual learning experience might support students' skill development. We selected two classes of special education students to participate in our study: one in Pittsburgh and the other in Nebraska. The teachers were enthusiastic to use the Hocus Focus curriculum to develop communication, fine motor, and social skills in their students. I was intrigued by the components necessary to teach and learn a magic trick through modeling and how the development of cognitive skills for retention was achieved through distance education.

During our first session I noticed a girl tucked into the back corner of the room with body language indicating that *she* wanted to disappear. Her hair was drawn over her face, hoodie up, arms crossed, slouching uncomfortably in her chair—she indicated clearly that she was not excited to participate. As the session began and Kevin popped onto the screen, his experience as an entertainer quickly gained the attention of the students. He made sure that each child felt seen offering comments to engage them often injecting humor in his delivery. However, the student in the corner continued her sulking behavior. However, over the 12-week period of the project —we met once a week— Kevin eventually melted even our reluctant learner's resolve to self-isolate.

Miraculously, on the last day of our program, we were all amazed when the student jumped up in front of the camera to show the class in Nebraska how to perform the last trick. Her enthusiasm and positive energy were transformational for me as I observed the power of teaching like a magician. From that day on, I was sold! I've learned so much from Kevin which expanded my teaching style and can testify that the results are amazing. I am excited that he has decided to share some of his teaching 'secrets' with teachers interested in creating a more engaging and purposeful learning environment.

Susan L. O'Rourke, Ed.D.
Professor Emeritus
Carlow University, PA

Meet the Author

Kevin Spencer

Dr. Kevin Spencer.
Photograph by Mike Turner.

Kevin Spencer, Ph.D., is an award-winning performing artist who, for more than 25 years, toured the world with one of the largest and most successful theatrical illusion productions in the U.S. He and his wife left behind a trail of accolades in their wake including 2009 *International Illusionist of the Year*, 2015 *International Magician of the Year*, and six-time recipient of *Performing Arts Entertainer of the Year*.

At the pinnacle of his career, Spencer stepped away from the stage and into classrooms and hospitals. As an educator, artist, consultant, and cultural entrepreneur, he works to create inclusive communities where everyone experiences an authentic sense of belonging and no one—for any reason—is relegated to the margins.

His work focuses on using the art of magic to impact change in the lives of children with autism, developmental disabilities, intellectual challenges, emotional behavior disorders, and those who have experienced trauma. He has dedicated thousands of hours inspiring students in classrooms across the globe, turning everyday lessons into unforgettable learning experiences. His program—Hocus Focus™—is a 2020 nominee for the Zero Project Award which recognizes innovative practices and models that improve the daily lives of persons with disabilities.

Spencer is a leading voice in the performing arts industry, a Fulbright Specialist on arts integration for special populations for the U.S. Department of State, faculty in the department of education at Carlow University in Pittsburgh, a research consultant for the Occupational Therapy department and Institute of Arts in Medicine at the University of Alabama at Birmingham, and an Approved Provider of Continuing Education for the American Occupational Therapy Association. He has earned a B.S. in Psychology and an M.Ed. in Arts Integration, and is a Ph.D. candidate in special education.

In 2014, he produced a short documentary—*Powerful Medicine: Simply Magic*—that showcases individuals of varying abilities who, through the art of magic, have overcome physical, developmental, and intellectual challenges. It has earned 18 international film festival awards and continues to inspire audiences around the world.

Kevin Spencer has dedicated his life to making a difference in communities around the world—both on and off the stage. He is a thought leader who addresses the inequality of individuals with disabilities with creativity, confidence, and courage.

Why Did I Write This Book?

Thank you for picking up this book. Perhaps the title caught your attention, or maybe you were searching for fresh, practical ways to re-engage your students in meaningful learning. Whatever led you here, I'm truly grateful—and confident that what you'll find in these pages is grounded in research, shaped by real-world experience, and designed with educators like you in mind.

Many of my colleagues who know my story have said it's closely woven into the content and context of this book. And they're right. My journey into education was anything but traditional—I came to the classroom later in life, entering the field as a second career. What surprised me most, though, is how valuable my first career turned out to be in shaping the educator I've become.

When I was nine, I received a magic set for Christmas. I had been fascinated by the magicians I'd watched on TV and told my mom, *"When I grow up, I'm going to be a magician."* I practiced every trick in that set relentlessly, performing for friends, classmates, and anyone who'd watch. While music eventually became my main focus in high school, magic always remained close by—quietly influencing how I saw the world and how I connected with others.

I pursued music in college, planning to become a concert pianist. But partway through, my passion for magic resurfaced. I took a job at a local magic shop, where I was introduced to new effects and fresh approaches to performance. I started doing shows on campus and around town—and before long, I found myself wondering, *Could this actually be a career?*

I changed my major from music to psychology, thinking that if I was going to work with perception and wonder, I should understand the mind behind it. After graduating, I poured myself into creating a full-stage magic show. When we felt we were ready, my wife, Cindy, and I launched a cabaret-style act that toured college campuses across the country.

From the very beginning, our focus was never just on tricks—it was always on connection. We believed that strong magic should be paired with even stronger personality. That approach struck a chord with audiences and led to several honors, including *Campus Entertainers of the Year* (we even beat out the Indigo Girls for that one!), *Best Variety Artists*, *Best Major Production*, and *Performing Arts Entertainers of the Year* (for six consecutive years).

Then, just as we were reaching the peak of our college career, everything changed. I was involved in a serious auto accident—my car was struck and crushed by a tractor-trailer. I woke up in neurological intensive care with a closed brain injury and a lower spinal cord injury. What followed were months of rehabilitation as I worked to regain basic skills. My fine motor skills were clumsy, my coordination unsteady, and even walking independently became a goal I had to work toward again. It was a difficult, frustrating, and—to be honest—often boring process. But thanks to the dedication of the therapists and medical professionals around me, I stayed motivated and made a full recovery. That experience gave me a profound new perspective. I became acutely aware of the daily realities faced by people with disabilities—the frustration, the barriers, and especially the limitations that others often place on them. I came to understand something essential: people with disabilities will only rise as high as we allow them. They have the same hopes and dreams as each one of us—but their futures are often shaped by our perceptions and attitudes about who they are and what they are capable of doing.

That realization shifted everything for me. Drawing on my experience as a performer and a patient, I began collaborating with therapists to develop a new approach to rehabilitation: using simple magic tricks as a motivating, hands-on way to help patients improve cognitive and motor skills. What started as a creative experiment soon grew into a research-supported program. The American Occupational Therapy Association supports the use of magic tricks as an authentic therapeutic tool, and today, the principles of what's now known as *magic therapy*® are being used in thousands of hospitals, clinics, schools, and rehabilitation centers around the world.

Once I recovered, my career as a touring illusionist didn't stop. As the show grew in both size and scope, we transitioned from college campuses to performing arts centers. It wasn't exactly starting over, but it did require adapting our strategies to meet a different market. Along the way, we rebranded from *The Magic of Kevin Spencer* to *Spencers' Theatre of Illusion*, evolving into a high-energy fusion of rock & roll and Broadway. The production struck a chord with audiences worldwide, and through it all, personality remained at the heart of the show.

For more than 20 years, we were the largest theatrical touring illusion show in the USA, traveling the world and performing on some of the most spectacular stages in the USA, Europe, and Asia. Along the way, we were honored as the 2009 *International Magicians of the Year* and received the 2015 *Illusionist Award* from the Milbourne Christopher Foundation for our significant contributions to the art of magic.

It had been an incredible journey, but in 2015, we made a pivotal decision—to retire the illusion show and redirect our passion for magic toward a new purpose: empowering children and adolescents with special education needs to strengthen both their academic and functional skills through the transformative power of a magic trick. By that point, we had experienced two very distinct seasons in our lives, and we were preparing to step into a third. I went back to school and earned my Master's degree in *Arts and Interdisciplinary Academic Education* and my Ph.D. in *Education* with an emphasis on special education. What I didn't realize then was how much my experiences—of crafting wonder, engaging an audience, reading a room, and adapting in real time—would prepare me for the classroom. And by incorporating the research-based educational framework of Universal Design for Learning (UDL), I realized I could design inclusive learning experiences that would accommodate the full range of learner variability adeptly meeting the needs of all learners regardless of grade level or ability.

In many ways, teaching is its own form of magic: it's about creating moments of surprise, curiosity, and connection that make learning come alive. I combined what I had learned with

FIGURE 0.1 Dr. Kevin Spencer laughs with a female student during the performance of a magic trick. Photo by Geri Kodey.

my love for the art of illusion and developed an innovative supplemental curriculum called *Hocus Focus*™. This is a creative instructional approach to support the learning of students with varying degrees of educational challenges and abilities.

Engagement, motivation, curiosity, and joy—these are the heartbeats of both performance and education. Today, I have shifted my focus entirely to using simple magic tricks as a tool to create meaningful change in the lives of children and adolescents with autism, developmental disabilities, intellectual challenges, emotional disturbances, and histories of trauma. What started as a passion for performance has now become a mission—one that continues to inspire and challenge me every day.

That's the heart of this book: how we, as educators, can design experiences that captivate, inspire, and truly engage our students—all of our students including those with special education needs. I'm excited to share what I've learned. My hope is that these ideas will help you rekindle a sense of wonder in your classroom and connect with your students in ways that are both meaningful and transformative.

Introducing *Teach Like a Magician*
Unveiling the Enchanting Art of Education

What does it mean to teach like a magician? After spending over 10,000 hours in classrooms with students of all ages and abilities, I've delved deeply into the techniques, skills, behaviors, habits, and approaches that shape effective teaching. For several years, I also taught a university-level course for pre-service teachers, where we explored the intersection of the arts and disability. The acronym **MAGICIAN** represents eight research-based practices that are essential for improving student engagement and learning, particularly in challenging educational settings. Each letter stands for a key strategy that enhances the learning experience.

- **M** stands for Motivation, emphasizing the importance of fostering intrinsic drive.
- **A** represents Active Learning, promoting hands-on, interactive methods.
- **G** highlights Goal-Directed Instruction, focusing on clear, achievable learning objectives.
- **I** refers to Imaginative Teaching, which encourages creativity and critical thinking.
- **C** stands for Curiosity, an essential component of fostering a love for learning.
- **I** also represents Immersion, which emphasizes being fully present and engaged with students.
- **A** stands for Affirmation, underscoring the value of positive reinforcement.

- Finally, **N** represents Natural Rapport, the importance of building genuine, trusting relationships with students. Together, these practices form a comprehensive approach to creating a dynamic and supportive learning environment that promotes academic success and personal growth.

Education is a transformative process that shapes individuals, empowers societies, and paves the way for a brighter future. Throughout history, various teaching methodologies have emerged, each with its unique approach to capturing students' attention, fostering engagement, and facilitating learning. Among these approaches, one metaphorical concept stands out: "Teach like a magician." This notion evokes the idea of educators embracing the enchanting and captivating qualities of magicians to create awe-inspiring and impactful teaching experiences. By exploring the parallels between teaching and magic, we uncover a profound understanding of the art of education.

The Personality of Presentation

Teaching like a magician entails incorporating elements of showmanship and charisma into the educational process. Similar to magicians who captivate their audience with sleight of hand and compelling narratives, educators can employ various techniques to engage students actively. By infusing enthusiasm, energy, and passion into their teaching style, teachers can create an immersive learning environment that enthralls students' attention. The art of captivating storytelling, the clever use of visual aids, and the skillful utilization of body language can all contribute to a teacher's charismatic presentation. By harnessing these techniques, educators can create an atmosphere where students eagerly anticipate each lesson, promoting deep learning and knowledge retention.

The Power of Illusion

Magicians are known for their ability to create illusions that challenge perception and logic. In the realm of education, teachers can leverage this concept to encourage critical thinking, problem-solving, and creativity. By presenting students with thought-provoking scenarios, paradoxes, and puzzling questions, educators can stimulate curiosity and inspire students to explore alternative perspectives. This approach helps students develop analytical skills, question assumptions, and engage in higher-order thinking. Moreover, teachers can employ the notion of illusion to demystify complex concepts, breaking them down into simpler components and offering analogies or metaphors that make them more accessible to learners.

The Element of Surprise

One of the key aspects of magic lies in its ability to surprise and delight the audience. Similarly, teachers can employ surprise elements in their instructional strategies to enhance engagement and foster a sense of wonder in the classroom. This can involve unexpected demonstrations, interactive activities, or unexpected twists in the learning process. By introducing unpredictability and novelty into their teaching methods, educators create a dynamic learning environment that encourages active participation and heightens students' curiosity. These surprise elements can also serve as memorable hooks that anchor learning experiences in students' minds, facilitating long-term knowledge retention.

The Transformational Impact

Magic performances often leave audiences with a sense of amazement and a lasting impact. Likewise, teachers who adopt the "Teach like a magician" approach aim to create transformative learning experiences that leave a lasting impression on their students. By infusing passion, creativity, and innovation into their teaching, educators can inspire and empower learners, instilling a love for lifelong learning. The magical approach emphasizes the importance of fostering individual strengths, encouraging self-expression, and nurturing a growth mindset. It also emphasizes the role of teachers as facilitators, guiding students on a journey of discovery and unlocking their full potential.

Summary

The concept of "Teach like a magician" encapsulates the essence of creating extraordinary educational experiences that captivate, inspire, and empower learners. By embracing the qualities of charisma, illusion, surprise, and transformation, educators can reimagine their roles as "magicians" in the classroom. This approach encourages them to explore innovative teaching methods, engage students on a deeper level, and facilitate meaningful learning experiences. Teaching like a magician goes beyond the transfer of knowledge; it encompasses the art of awakening curiosity, fostering critical thinking, and igniting a lifelong passion for learning. By blending the magic of education with the enchantment of performance, educators can create an educational landscape that embraces imagination, wonder, and the limitless potential of human growth.

1

M is for Motivation

Education is not the filling of a pail, but the lighting of a fire.
—William Butler Yeats, Irish Poet and Nobel Laureate

Motivation drives behavior and achievement, serving as the foundation for learning and teaching. **Teacher motivation** primarily stems from intrinsic factors like passion for education, desire to make a difference, and personal growth, as well as extrinsic factors such as salary, recognition, and professional development. Motivated teachers are more likely to inspire students, connect with them in meaningful ways, create engaging lessons, and foster a positive classroom environment.

In contrast, **student motivation** revolves around the desire to learn, influenced by intrinsic curiosity, relevance of the material, or extrinsic rewards like grades and praise. While teachers often focus on enabling others, students aim to fulfill personal goals or societal expectations.

The critical difference lies in their objectives: teacher motivation sustains the *delivery of knowledge*, while student motivation *drives the pursuit* of knowledge. Recognizing this distinction allows educators to tailor their approaches, ensuring that their enthusiasm cultivates an engaging atmosphere that nurtures student curiosity and commitment.

Teacher Motivation

Teacher motivation is fundamental to the overall effectiveness and quality of education. A motivated teacher brings energy, dedication, and creativity to their profession, which directly impacts their own professional satisfaction and growth. When teachers are driven, they are more likely to approach their work with enthusiasm and resilience, even in the face of challenges such as limited resources or administrative demands.

Motivated teachers engage in continuous learning and self-improvement, seeking opportunities for professional development to stay updated with the latest educational practices and technologies. This enhances their ability to teach effectively and adapt to diverse classroom needs. Furthermore, teacher motivation fosters a sense of purpose and commitment, which can reduce burnout and increase job retention, ensuring a stable and experienced workforce in schools.

Ultimately, motivated teachers are pivotal in shaping the broader educational landscape, advocating for innovations, and contributing to policies that improve teaching conditions and learning outcomes. Teacher motivation plays a crucial role in shaping the quality and effectiveness of the education system. It directly influences teachers' professional behaviors, job satisfaction, and overall well-being, which are essential for creating a sustainable and impactful teaching career. The significance of teacher motivation can be explored through its impact on professional development, workplace engagement, and long-term career commitment.

Professional Development and Growth (Hafiz et al., 2021). Motivated teachers are proactive in seeking opportunities for professional growth. They actively engage in workshops, training sessions, and self-directed learning to refine their teaching methodologies and stay abreast of new developments in pedagogy and subject matter. This continuous learning not only enhances their expertise but also fosters innovation in the classroom. Teachers who are motivated often go beyond routine expectations, exploring creative solutions to educational challenges and adopting new technologies and strategies to improve their instructional approaches.

Workplace Engagement and Enthusiasm (Dreer, 2021; Heim & Marshall, 2022). A motivated teacher approaches their role with enthusiasm and dedication. This positivity is reflected in their ability to manage classroom dynamics effectively, establish strong relationships with colleagues, and contribute meaningfully to school-wide initiatives. Motivated teachers tend to collaborate more willingly with peers, sharing ideas and resources that benefit the entire school community. Their engagement extends beyond classroom teaching to include participation in curriculum design, mentorship programs, and extracurricular activities, further enriching the educational environment.

Resilience and Adaptability (Beltman & Poulton, 2025). The teaching profession can be demanding, with challenges ranging from administrative pressures to balancing diverse student needs. Motivation serves as a buffer, helping teachers navigate these difficulties with resilience. A motivated teacher is more likely to view challenges as opportunities for growth rather than obstacles. This mindset fosters adaptability, enabling teachers to adjust their strategies to meet the evolving demands of their roles and the changing educational landscape.

Job Satisfaction and Retention (Chang & Sung, 2024; Yildiz & Kiliç, 2021). Teacher motivation is closely tied to job satisfaction. When educators feel motivated, they experience a greater sense of fulfillment in their work, which contributes to their overall happiness and mental health. This satisfaction reduces the likelihood of burnout, a common issue in the teaching profession, and promotes long-term career commitment. Retaining motivated teachers is critical for maintaining stability within schools, as it reduces turnover and ensures the continuity of quality teaching.

Advocacy and Leadership (Coggins & McGovern, 2014; Lovett, 2023). Motivated teachers often emerge as leaders and advocates within the education system. Their passion and drive inspire them to take on leadership roles, such as department heads or curriculum developers, where they can influence broader educational practices. They are also more likely to advocate for policies and reforms that improve teaching conditions, enhance educational resources, and address systemic challenges. This leadership helps to elevate the teaching profession and contributes to the advancement of education as a whole.

Student Motivation

Student motivation is a vital factor in the educational process, shaping how learners approach their studies, overcome challenges, and achieve academic and personal goals. It is the driving force behind engagement, persistence, and the desire to acquire knowledge and skills. Understanding and fostering student motivation is crucial for creating a learning environment that promotes growth, curiosity, and achievement.

Encourages Active Participation (Boncquet et al., 2024). Motivated students are more likely to actively engage in the learning process, whether through classroom discussions, group projects, or individual assignments. They take initiative in their studies, asking questions, seeking clarity, and exploring topics beyond the curriculum. This active participation not only enhances their understanding of the material but also cultivates critical thinking and problem-solving skills that are essential for lifelong learning.

Supports Goal Achievement (Khan et al., 2024; Taylor et al., 2014). Motivation provides the drive students need to set and achieve academic and personal goals. Intrinsic motivation, which comes from within the learner, fosters a love for learning and curiosity about the world. Extrinsic motivation, such as the desire for good grades or recognition, can also play a significant role in encouraging students to work hard. Both forms of motivation help students maintain focus and perseverance, even when faced with challenges or setbacks.

Builds Resilience and Perseverance (Dweck & Yeager, 2019; Rattan et al., 2012; Yeager & Dweck, 2012; Zhao et al., 2024). The journey of learning is often fraught with obstacles, from difficult concepts to external pressures. Motivation helps students build resilience, enabling them to push through these difficulties and maintain their effort over time. Psychologist Carol Dweck introduced the concept of Growth Mindset, the belief that intelligence and abilities can be developed through effort, effective strategies, and input from others. According to Dweck, motivated students with a growth mindset are more likely to view failures as opportunities to learn and grow, rather than as insurmountable barriers. Students who believe their abilities can grow are more likely to engage in learning strategies, seek feedback, and recover from failure constructively. And teachers who promote a growth-oriented classroom culture—emphasizing learning over performance—help students develop more adaptive approaches to learning. This perseverance is critical not only for academic success but also for developing the grit required to navigate challenges in other areas of life.

Enhances Academic Performance (Buzdar et al., 2017; Sharma & Sharma, 2018; Sivrikaya, 2019). Motivated students typically perform better academically. They are more likely to complete assignments on time, prepare thoroughly for exams, and stay organized in their studies. Motivation drives them to seek resources, manage their time effectively, and take ownership of their learning journey. As a result, they often achieve higher grades and a deeper understanding of the subject matter.

Promotes Personal Development (Frade et al., 2017). Beyond academics, motivation plays a key role in shaping a student's personal development. It encourages them to explore their interests, develop new skills, and build self-confidence. Motivated students are more likely to participate in extracurricular activities, volunteer work, or internships, all of which contribute to their holistic growth and future readiness.

Prepares for Future Challenges (Frade et al., 2017. The skills and habits developed through sustained motivation—such as time management, goal setting, and self-discipline—are invaluable in preparing students for future academic, professional, and personal challenges. Motivation instills a sense of purpose and direction, helping students navigate transitions and adapt to the demands of higher education, the workforce, or other pursuits.

Bringing Learning to Life

When I first began working with students many years ago, I was filled with enthusiasm and a deep passion for creating a space where children could truly fall in love with learning. I was a highly motivated educator, eager to make a difference from day 1.

During my first week, I was asked to work with a particular student—a nine-year-old boy named Thomas. He had some minor fine motor challenges, but it was clear he was intelligent and observant. What I didn't realize at the time was that Thomas would also be my first encounter with a child on the autism spectrum.

I decided to spend a few minutes one-on-one with him—just 15–20 minutes. During that short session, I performed a simple magic trick. Thomas watched quietly, intently focused. When I finished, he looked at me and asked if I could teach him how to do it. I handed him a small piece of rope and began to guide him through the steps. The questions came quickly: "How do I hold the rope?" "Where do I put my hands?" "How do I cross my arms?" He was excited and engaged, and to his delight, he successfully performed the trick on his very first try. The pride on his face was unmistakable. He repeated the trick several times, joyfully sharing it with the occupational and speech therapists who were in the room with us.

In just a few minutes, a genuine connection had formed. That brief interaction laid the foundation of trust and rapport—giving Thomas the confidence to explore, engage, and communicate. We talked about the science behind the trick and, along the way, reinforced key concepts like basic prepositions: up/down, top/bottom, over/under, and left/right. Throughout the session, Thomas remained actively involved and conversational.

It wasn't until later, in a conversation with his speech therapist, that I learned Thomas was selectively mute. She shared that she had never heard him speak in full sentences before and wasn't certain he had the capacity to do so. She had certainly never heard him ask so many questions.

This experience has stayed with me as a powerful reminder that student motivation is deeply tied to curiosity, relevance, and the opportunity for meaningful connection. When students are curious, when learning feels relevant, and when there's a safe space to explore, motivation naturally follows. And motivation is the key driver of engagement, persistence, and the desire to grow.

Summary

Teacher and student motivation are essential for effective learning and educational success. Teacher motivation drives enthusiasm, innovation, and professional growth, ensuring engaging and high-quality instruction. It fosters resilience and long-term commitment, which are critical for sustaining a thriving educational environment. Student motivation, on the other hand, propels active participation, perseverance, and academic achievement. It builds resilience, encourages personal growth, and prepares learners for future challenges. Together, these motivations create a dynamic and inspiring educational setting where teaching and learning flourish. Prioritizing motivation in both teachers and students is key to fostering curiosity, engagement, and success in the learning journey.

Discussion Questions

1. What are some strategies you can implement to sustain and enhance your motivation, particularly in under-resourced or high-pressure environments?
2. How can you effectively balance intrinsic and extrinsic motivators in the classroom to support diverse student needs and learning goals?
3. In what ways does your motivation impact the long-term academic and emotional outcomes of students, especially those in special education programs?
4. Considering the distinct motivations of teachers and students, how can you design instruction that aligns your own passion for teaching with students' personal goals and interests?
5. How does motivation—both for teachers and for students—serve as a protective factor against burnout, disengagement, or dropout in educational settings?

References

Beltman, S., & Poulton, E. (2025). Strategies teachers use to maintain motivation. *Teaching and Teacher Education, 155*, 104882. https://doi.org/10.1016/j.tate.2024.104882.

Boncquet, M., Flamant, N., Lavrijsen, J., Vansteenkiste, M., Verschueren, K., & Soenens, B. (2024). The unique importance of motivation and mindsets for students' learning behavior and achievement: An examination at the level of between-student differences and within-student fluctuations. *Journal of Educational Psychology, 116*(3), 448–465. https://doi.org/10.1037/edu0000827

Buzdar, M. A., Mohsin, M. N., Akbar, R., & Mohammad, N. (2017). Students' academic performance and its relationship with their intrinsic and extrinsic motivation. *Journal of Educational Research, 20*(1), 74.

Chang, T. J., & Sung, Y. T. (2024). Does teacher motivation really matter? Exploring the mediating role of teachers' self-efficacy in the relationship between motivation and job satisfaction. *The Asia-Pacific Education Researcher, 33*, 1315–1325. https://doi.org/10.1007/s40299-023-00803-4

Coggins, C., & McGovern, K. (2014). Five goals for teacher leadership. *The Phi Delta Kappan, 95*(7), 15–21. https://www.jstor.org/stable/24374713

Dreer, B. (2021). Teachers' well-being and job satisfaction: The important role of positive emotions in the workplace. *Educational Studies, 50*(1), 61–77. https://doi.org/10.1080/03055698.2021.1940872

Dweck, C. S., & Yeager, D. S. (2019). Mindsets: A view from two eras. *Perspectives on Psychological Science, 14*(3), 481–496.

Frade, A. S. B. V., Veiga, F. H., Sílvia Bernardo Vinhas Frade, A., & Veiga, F. H. (2017). Student motivation and self-concept: Is there a connection? *European Proceedings of Social and Behavioural Sciences, 31*, 203–213.

Hafiz, N. A., Ali, R. P., & Malik, M. (2021). The role of teacher training programs in optimizing teacher motivation and professional development skills. *Bulletin of Education and Research, 43*(2), 17. https://www.proquest.com/scholarly-journals/role-teacher-training-programs-optimizing/docview/2680023346/se-2

Heim, K., & Marshall, K. (2022). Reframing teacher engagement: A framework for improving workplace conditions to foster teacher engagement. *Alberta Journal of Educational Research, 68*(4), 561–580. https://doi.org/10.11575/ajer.v68i4.74708.

Khan, W., Saeed, M. R., Khan, H., & Lee, R. (2024, December). How teacher behaviour influences learning performance: The mediating role of student motivation. *Perspectives in Education*, 42(4), 39–53. https://doi.org/10.38140/pie.v42i4.7193

Lovett, S. (2023). Teacher leadership and teachers' learning: Actualizing the connection from day one. *Professional Development in Education*, 49(6), 1010–1021. https://doi.org/10.1080/19415257.2023.2235583

Rattan, A., Good, C., & Dweck, C. S. (2012). "It's OK – Not Everyone Can Be Good at Math": Instructors with an entity theory comfort (and demotivate) students. *Journal of Experimental Social Psychology*, 48(3), 731–737. https://doi.org/10.1016/j.jesp.2011.12.012

Sharma, D., & Sharma, S. (2018). Relationship between motivation and academic achievement. *International Journal of Advances in Scientific Research*, 4(1), 1–5. https://www.semanticscholar.org/paper/Relationship-between-motivation-and-academic-Sharma-Sharma/bd1183ff9d89a8621f6ee25cb121504c6d265b46

Sivrikaya, A. H. (2019). The relationship between academic motivation and academic achievement of the students. *Asian Journal of Education and Training*, 5(2), 309–315. https://doi.org/10.20448/journal.522.2019.52.309.315

Taylor, G., Jungert, T., Mageau, G. A., Schatke, K., Dedic, H., Rosenfield, S., & Koestner, R. (2014). A self-determination theory approach to predicting school achievement over time: The unique role of intrinsic motivation. *Contemporary Educational Psychology.*, 39(4), 342–358. https://doi.org/10.1016/j.cedpsych.2014.08.002

Yeager, D. S., & Dweck, C. S. (2012). Mindsets that promote resilience: When students believe that personal characteristics can be developed. *Educational Psychologist*, 47(4), 302–314.

Yildiz, V. A., & Kiliç, D. (2021). Investigation of the relationship between class teachers' motivation and job satisfaction. *International Online Journal of Education and Teaching*, 8(1), 119–131.

Zhao, W., Shi, X., Jin, M., Li, Y., Liang, C., Ji, Y., Cao, J., Oubibi, M., Li, X., & Tian, Y. (2024). The impact of a growth mindset on high school students' learning subjective well-being: The serial mediation role of achievement motivation and grit. *Frontiers in Psychology*, 15, 1399343. https://doi.org/10.3389/fpsyg.2024.1399343.

2

A is for Active Learning

> The mediocre teacher tells. The good teacher explains. The superior teacher demonstrates. The great teacher inspires.
> —William Arthur Ward, Educator and Author

Active learning fosters deeper understanding, encourages problem-solving, and builds critical life skills by tailoring instruction to meet individual needs. Moreover, it creates an inclusive environment where students feel empowered, respected, and motivated, making it a cornerstone of effective education practices.

The Value and Implementation of Active Learning in the Classroom

Active learning is an instructional approach that prioritizes engagement, interaction, and participation over passive consumption of knowledge. It is particularly valuable in special education classrooms, where diverse needs, learning styles, and abilities demand customized and responsive teaching strategies. By fostering hands-on, experiential, and collaborative learning opportunities, active learning creates a supportive environment that nurtures students' academic, social, and emotional growth (Doolittle et al., 2023). This detailed exploration highlights the significance of active learning for diverse learners and provides practical strategies for its implementation.

The Value of Active Learning

Engagement and Motivation (Odum et al., 2021). Active learning captivates students' attention by involving them directly in the learning process. Activities such as problem-solving tasks, role-playing, or group discussions make lessons more engaging than traditional lectures. In special education, where students may struggle with attention or motivation, this participatory approach is particularly effective in maintaining focus and enthusiasm for learning.

Accommodating Diverse Learning Needs (Munna & Kalam, 2021). Every student in a classroom learns differently. Students with special education needs often require individualized approaches. Active learning offers flexibility, allowing educators to adapt activities to students' strengths, needs, and preferred learning modalities, whether visual, auditory, kinesthetic, or a combination. For example, tactile learners may benefit from manipulatives, while auditory learners may excel through verbal discussions.

Promoting Critical Thinking and Problem-Solving Skills (Kusumoto, 2018). Active learning encourages students to analyze, evaluate, and apply knowledge rather than merely memorizing it. This approach fosters critical thinking, problem-solving, and decision-making, which are essential life skills. In special education, active learning can be structured to teach functional skills, such as budgeting through real-world math scenarios or social skills through role-playing exercises.

Building Social and Emotional Skills (Casciano et al., 2019; CASEL, 2005; Green et al., 2021). Social Emotional Learning (SEL) equips individuals with the skills to recognize and manage emotions, build healthy relationships, make responsible decisions, and handle challenges effectively. Its value lies in fostering emotional intelligence, improving academic performance, enhancing mental well-being, and promoting positive behavior—laying the foundation for lifelong success in both personal and professional spheres. Many students in special education programs require support in developing social and emotional competencies. Active learning often involves collaboration and communication, providing opportunities for students to work together, share ideas, and practice empathy. Group activities help build confidence, teamwork, and interpersonal skills that are crucial for navigating real-life situations.

Encouraging Independence and Empowerment (Bezerra et al., 2024). Active learning shifts responsibility from the teacher to the student, empowering learners to take ownership of their education. In a special education context, this fosters self-confidence and autonomy. For instance, allowing students to choose activities or solve problems independently reinforces a sense of control, autonomy, and accomplishment, building their self-esteem. Other examples would include:

- *Student-Created Performances:* Students write, rehearse, and perform skits or short plays to demonstrate understanding of a topic (e.g., historical events, science concepts, social-emotional themes) to build collaboration and communication and develop a deeper comprehension of the content.
- *Genius Hour | Passion Projects:* Students choose a topic they're passionate about, research it, and present their findings in creative ways (videos, posters, presentations, etc.) to promote autonomy, curiosity, and research skills.
- *Peer Teaching:* Students take turn teaching mini-lessons to the class on a topic they've mastered reinforcing the content while building confidence and leadership skills.
- *Inquiry-Based Projects:* Students design and carry out their own experiments based on questions they create, then analyze and present their results to support critical thinking and hands-on learning.
- *Student-Led Conferences:* Instead of parent-teacher conferences, students present their learning progress, goals, and reflections to their parents and teachers encouraging ownership and self-awareness.

Enhancing Retention and Transfer of Knowledge (Chi & Wylie, 2014). When students actively engage with material through application, discussion, or experimentation, they are more likely to understand and retain the information. Active learning also facilitates the transfer of knowledge to new contexts, enabling students to apply what they learn in the classroom to real-world situations.

Implementation of Active Learning

Implementing active learning in the classroom requires intentional planning, creativity, and a thorough understanding of students' individual needs and abilities. Below are strategies and considerations for effective implementation:

Start with Clear Objectives (Zaur, 2021). Active learning activities should align with specific educational goals, such as improving literacy, developing problem-solving skills, or enhancing social communication. Establishing clear objectives ensures that activities remain purposeful and focused on outcomes that benefit students' development. Here are some examples of how this can be done:

Write Objectives on the Board and Review Daily

- How to do it: At the start of class, write the day's objective in student-friendly language.
- Add engagement: Ask a student volunteer to read it aloud and rephrase it in their own words.
- Connect to purpose: Ask, "Why might this be important to us today?" to spark relevance.

Show an Overview of the Unit with Checkpoints

- How to do it: Create a visual map or timeline of the unit and display it in class or digitally.
- Add checkpoints: Include "goalposts"—mini-objectives or performance tasks that students will complete.
- Make it student-facing: Use icons, visuals, or symbols to show progress and keep students oriented.

Use "What Are We Learning?" and "How Will We Know?" Prompts

- How to do it: At the beginning of each lesson, post two simple questions:
  - "What are we learning today?"
  - "How will we know we've learned it?"
- Student ownership: Have students write or verbalize their own answers at the start and reflect again at the end of the lesson.

Align Active Learning with Objectives: For Each Activity, Explicitly Link the Student-Led Task to the Objective

- Example for Magic Trick Demo (Fine Motor + Communication):
  - Objective: "I can demonstrate a learned skill and clearly explain the steps involved."
  - Before activity: "Today's trick is about clear sequencing and storytelling—both are communication goals!"
  - After activity: "How did this help us meet our objective? What can we do better next time?"

Reflect and Revisit Objectives

- Use exit tickets or journals where students finish the sentence:
  - "Today I learned..." or
  - "I'm getting better at..."
- Revisit the unit overview and let students self-check or color in checkpoints as they meet them.

Use Visual Cues or Icons

Especially for younger students or those in special education, using meaningful symbols—such as a lightbulb to signify learning, a compass to indicate direction, and a checkmark to mark goals achieved—can help make learning objectives feel more tangible and attainable.

Incorporate Multisensory Approaches (Abdulla & Eissa, 2019; Maliki & Yasin, 2017). Students—especially special education students—often benefit from multisensory experiences that engage multiple senses simultaneously. Activities like using textured letters for spelling, creating art projects to illustrate concepts, or participating in movement-based math games can make abstract ideas more concrete and accessible.

Utilize Assistive Technology (Bell, 2023; CTI, n.d.). Technology plays a significant role in facilitating active learning for students, especially learners with diverse needs. Tools such as interactive whiteboards, speech-to-text software, and adaptive learning apps allow students to participate in ways that accommodate their abilities. For example, a student with limited mobility might use a touch-screen device to complete a science experiment simulation.

Encourage Peer Collaboration (Cheetham & Varga-Atkins, 2021; Mendo et al., 2018). Group work and peer-led activities are essential components of active learning. Structured collaboration can help students of all abilities practice social skills and learn from one another's strengths. For instance, pairing students with complementary abilities for a project fosters teamwork and mutual support.

Incorporate Real-World Applications (Education World, n.d.; Fink, 2022; Michigan State University Ext, 2015; Rutgers NJAES, n.d.). Active learning becomes particularly meaningful when tied to real-world scenarios. Classrooms can incorporate activities like cooking to teach math and reading skills, gardening to teach science, or navigating public transportation maps to enhance spatial awareness and independence. Such activities prepare students for everyday challenges outside the classroom.

Facilitate Reflection and Discussion (Pei et al., 2023). Reflection is a critical element of active learning. After completing an activity, students should have the opportunity to discuss their experiences, share what they learned, and connect it to their personal goals. This process reinforces understanding and helps educators assess the effectiveness of the activity.

Differentiate Activities (Langelaan et al., 2024). Given the range of abilities in inclusive classrooms, differentiation is key to successful active learning. Teachers can adapt tasks based on students' individual strengths and challenges, ensuring that each learner is appropriately challenged and supported. For instance, while one student may use flashcards to match vocabulary words, another may create sentences using the same words. Here are some additional examples:

Choice Boards / Menus

- ◆ Activity: Provide a menu of tasks for students to choose from, each targeting the same learning goal but in different formats (e.g., create a video, write an essay, build a model, and give a presentation).
- ◆ Differentiation: Students select a task based on their strengths, interests, and preferred mode of learning.

Example: In a history unit, students can choose between creating a diorama, writing a journal entry, making a podcast, or designing a timeline about a historical event.

Tiered Assignments

- ◆ Activity: Create assignments with varying levels of difficulty, but all designed to meet the same learning goal. Students work at the level that is most appropriate for their current understanding.
- ◆ Differentiation: Allows students to challenge themselves without feeling overwhelmed, and it gives those who need extra support a chance to succeed.

Example: In a math class, one group might solve simple problems with direct solutions, while another group solves complex word problems requiring multi-step strategies.

Peer Teaching

- Activity: Students are paired with peers of different skill levels. The more advanced student helps teach the material, while the other practices with guidance.
- Differentiation: This allows the teacher to focus on smaller groups and helps both students—the one teaching solidifies their understanding, while the one learning gets extra support.

Example: In a science class, students who grasp concepts faster can explain difficult experiments to classmates who need more support, reinforcing the learning for both.

Flexible Grouping

- Activity: Students are grouped dynamically based on their skill levels or interests, and the groups change over time. This provides opportunities for students to work with peers at different levels and from diverse perspectives.
- Differentiation: Helps create opportunities for collaboration while allowing students to engage with content in a variety of ways.

Example: In a literature class, a group of students might analyze a chapter together, while another group might focus on creative responses to the same text, like acting out scenes or creating artwork based on themes.

Gamification

- Activity: Incorporating game elements (e.g., points, levels, leaderboards, or badges) to incentivize progress. Students may complete activities at different paces but still aim toward the same learning goal.
- Differentiation: Different activities, challenges, or puzzles cater to diverse skills and knowledge levels, allowing students to progress at their own rate.

Example: In a language arts class, students play vocabulary games that vary in difficulty based on their proficiency level, allowing both advanced and struggling students to participate and succeed.

Scaffolding with Graphic Organizers

- Activity: Use graphic organizers (e.g., Venn diagrams, flowcharts, or concept maps) to help students visualize information.
- Differentiation: Provide simpler organizers for students who need more structure and more complex ones for students who are ready for deeper analysis.

Example: In a social studies unit, a student might use a simple Venn diagram to compare two cultures, while another student might use a more complex chart to explore deeper societal structures.

Audio/Visual Learning Tools

- Activity: Provide different modes of content delivery, such as audio recordings, video explanations, interactive apps, and hands-on experiments.
- Differentiation: Students who benefit from auditory or visual learning can access materials in a way that suits them best.

Example: In a math lesson, students can listen to an audio explanation of a concept, watch a tutorial video, or use a visual app to manipulate shapes and see math concepts in action.

Learning Stations

- Activity: Set up different stations that each focus on a different aspect of a lesson, such as reading comprehension, writing practice, and hands-on activities.
- Differentiation: Allows students to engage with content in multiple ways and at their own pace, while providing an opportunity for enrichment or review depending on needs.

Example: In a science unit, stations could include a lab activity, a reading passage with comprehension questions, and a creative project such as building a model of a cell.

Digital Platforms for Personalized Learning

- Activity: Use digital tools or platforms (like Google Classroom, Kahoot!, or adaptive learning programs like DreamBox) that allow students to engage with content in personalized ways.
- Differentiation: Technology can adapt in real time to a student's proficiency level, providing tailored content and feedback.

Example: In a reading program, students can read books at their appropriate level and complete quizzes that adjust to their comprehension, ensuring that they progress at their own pace.

Flexible Timing and Pacing

- Activity: Allow students to set their own pace within certain parameters, especially for projects or long-term assignments.
- Differentiation: Students who need more time or support can work at a slower pace, while others can move ahead or deepen their work without feeling held back.

Example: In a research project, students can choose their deadlines for milestones like the thesis statement, research outline, and final paper, allowing them to work at a pace that suits their individual needs.

Real-World Problem-Solving

- Activity: Engage students in solving real-world problems that allow for multiple solutions, emphasizing creativity, critical thinking, and collaboration.

♦ Differentiation: Different groups of students can tackle different aspects of the problem, based on their skills and strengths.

Example: In a business course, students might work on creating a marketing plan, with different students focusing on research, design, budgeting, and presentation, allowing for diverse contributions to a common goal.

Use Positive Reinforcement (Jula & Senados, 2023; Odum et al., 2021). Active learning thrives on a positive and supportive environment. Celebrate students' efforts and successes, providing specific feedback that reinforces their progress. Positive reinforcement not only boosts motivation but also encourages continued engagement in active learning activities.

Create Safe Spaces for Risk-Taking (Käfer et al., 2019). Active learning often involves experimentation and problem-solving, which can be intimidating for students. Establish a classroom culture that values effort and views mistakes as learning opportunities. This approach helps all students feel comfortable taking risks and exploring new ideas.

Involve Families and Caregivers (Hill & Tyson, 2009; Romero-González et al., 2023). Active learning doesn't have to be confined to the classroom. Involving families and caregivers in activities can extend learning to the home environment. Educators can provide resources and suggestions for hands-on learning at home, such as cooking, gardening, or community outings that reinforce classroom lessons.

Challenges and Solutions in Special Education

Implementing active learning in special education may come with challenges, such as managing diverse needs, limited resources, or time constraints. To address these:

♦ **Plan for Accessibility:** Ensure materials and activities are accessible to all students by incorporating universal design principles and using assistive tools where necessary.

- **Start Small:** Introduce active learning gradually, beginning with simple activities and building complexity as students and teachers become more comfortable.
- **Seek Professional Development:** Educators should pursue training to enhance their ability to design and implement active learning strategies tailored to special education. Exploring online resources like Empowered[1] or Solution Tree[2] are excellent places to begin.

Bringing Learning to Life

One of my greatest passions as an educator has always been creating inclusive learning experiences—bringing students of all abilities into the heart of the learning process. Having taught both general education and special education students, I've seen the incredible value in bringing these groups together in meaningful, shared experiences.

To bring this idea to life, I introduced a science-based activity to the high school Life Skills class—an engaging experiment with a seemingly impossible outcome. We rehearsed the activity several times, ensuring every student felt confident and had mastered the skills needed to teach it to someone else.

Once they were ready, we took it a step further. The Life Skills students became Subject Matter Experts and visited an AP Physics class. Each Life Skills student was paired with a small group of AP students. Their job? To teach the activity to their group. As the AP students learned the activity, they then worked to identify the physics vocabulary and formulas hidden within it.

But there was a twist—those advanced students had to explain their findings in language the Life Skills students could understand. This wasn't just about content knowledge; it was about communication, collaboration, and respect.

In this shared learning experience, everyone grew. The Life Skills students gained confidence, ownership, and a sense of leadership. The AP students deepened their understanding by teaching and adapting complex concepts in accessible ways. Active learning in this case didn't just enhance content knowledge—it promoted problem-solving, built critical communication skills, and met the diverse needs of every learner in the room.

Summary

Active learning is a transformative approach that values the unique abilities and needs of every student. By fostering engagement, independence, and meaningful learning experiences, active learning not only supports academic achievement but also prepares students for life beyond the classroom. With careful planning, adaptability, and a commitment to inclusivity, educators can create vibrant learning environments where all students thrive.

 **Discussion Questions**

1. How have you implemented active learning to support the development of both academic and life skills in students with diverse learning needs?
2. What are some effective strategies that you have implemented for differentiating active learning activities to meet the unique needs of each student?
3. In what ways can active learning promote social and emotional growth for students with disabilities, and in what way can you create safe spaces for risk-taking in this process?
4. How can assistive technology be integrated into active learning to increase accessibility and engagement for your students with physical, sensory, or cognitive challenges?
5. What role should families and caregivers play in reinforcing active learning at home, and how can you collaborate with them to support continuity and consistency?

Notes

1 https://teachempowered.org/
2 https://mkt.solutiontree.com/

References

Abdulla, M. A., & Eissa, M. A. (2019). Investigating the effect of multisensory approach on improving emergent literacy skills in children with autism spectrum disorder. *Topics in Early Childhood Special Education, 34*(3), 142–153.

Bell, J. (2023). *Using assistive technology for inclusive learning in K–12 classrooms*. IGI Global.

Bezerra, E. T., da Fonseca, J. R. M., Oliveira, I. dos S., Freitas, R. G., Fonsêca, J. R. M. da, Freitas, R. G., Lisboa, A. de O. C., Lima, I. F. dos santos, Vieira, A. J. F., Santos, M. de N. D. dos, Cruz, A. G. D. F. da, Scabeni, R. S., Celestino, E. M., & Damacena, R. (2024). Active methodologies and meaningful learning: Strategies to promote student engagement and autonomy. *Revista Foco, 17*(10), e6361. https://doi.org/10.54751/revistafoco.v17n10-022.

Casciano, R., Cherfas, L., & Jobson-Ahmed, L. (2019). Connecting arts integration to social-emotional learning among special education students. *Journal for Learning through the Arts, 15*(1), 4–25.

Cheetham, J., & Varga-Atkins, T. (2021). Designing peer learning groups and activities. University of Liverpool. Retrieved January 25, 2025, from https://www.liverpool.ac.uk/media/livacuk/centre-for-innovation-in-education/diy-guides/designing-peer-learning-groups-and-activities/designing-peer-learning-groups-and-activities.pdf

Chi, M. T., & Wylie, R. (2014). The ICAP framework: Linking cognitive engagement to active learning outcomes. *Educational Psychologist, 49*(4), 219–243.

Collaborative for Academic, Social, and Emotional Learning (CASEL). (2005). *Safe and sound: An educational leader's guide to evidence-based social and emotional learning (SEL) programs*. Chicago, IL: CASEL.

CTI. (n.d.). Assistive technology for special education – Enhancing access, engagement, and independence. CTI. Retrieved January 15, 2025, from https://www.cti.com/assistive-technology-for-special-education/

Doolittle, P., Wojdak, K., & Walters, A. (2023). Defining active learning: A restricted systematic review. *Teaching and Learning Inquiry, 11*, 6–9.

Education World. (n.d.). Simulations engage students in active learning. https://www.educationworld.com/a_curr/curr391.shtml

Fink, K. (2022, July 26). 16 everyday activities that count as learning. We Are Teachers. https://www.weareteachers.com/everyday-activities-that-count-as-learning

Green, A. L., Ferrante, S., Boaz, T. L., Kutash, K., & Wheeldon-Reece, B. (2021). Social and emotional learning during early adolescence: Effectiveness of a classroom-based SEL program for middle school students. *Psychology in the Schools, 58*(6), 1056–1069.

Hill, N. E., & Tyson, D. F. (2009). Parental involvement in middle school: A meta-analytic assessment of the strategies that promote academic achievement. *Developmental Psychology, 45*(3), 740–763. https://doi.org/10.1037/a0015362

Langelaan, B., Gaikhorst, L., Smets, W., & Oostdan, R. (2024). Differentiated instruction: Understanding the key elements for successful teacher preparation and development. *Teaching and Teacher Education, 140*, 104464. https://doi.org/10.1016/j.tate.2023.104464

Jula, N., & Senados, P. (2023). Positive reinforcement and its effect on students' classroom behavior and classroom work-related values. *Global Education Journal, 13*(1), 7–17. Retrieved from https://globusedujournal.in/wp-content/uploads/2023/03/GPE-131-JJ23-7.-Jula-Natassi-P.-Senados.pdf

Käfer, S., Tulis, M., & Kunter, M. (2019). The significance of dealing with mistakes for student motivation and learning. *European Journal of Psychology of Education, 34*(4), 731–753. https://link.springer.com/article/10.1007/s10212-018-0408-7

Kusumoto, Y. (2018). Enhancing critical thinking through active learning. *Language Learning in Higher Education, 8*(10), 45–63.

Maliki, N. S. M., & Yasin, M. H. M. (2017). Application of multisensory in learning alphabets identification skills for special education students. *Journal of ICSAR, 1*(2), 150–155.

Mendo, L., León, J., Felipe, E., Polo, M. I., & Fajardo, F. (2018). Cooperative team learning and the development of social skills in higher education: The variables involved. *Frontiers in Psychology, 9*, 1536. https://doi.org/10.3389/fpsyg.2018.01536

Michigan State University Extension. (2015, October 30). Making science concepts real with cooking and school gardens. https://www.canr.msu.edu/news/making_science_concepts_real_with_cooking_and_school_gardens

Munna, A. S., & Kalam, M. A. (2021). Impact of active learning strategy on the student engagement. *GNOSI: An Interdisciplinary Journal of Human Theory and Praxis, 4*(2), 96–114.

Odum, M., Meaney, K. S., & Knudson, D. V. (2021). Active learning classroom design and student engagement: An exploratory study. *Journal of Learning Spaces, 10*(1), 27–42. https://files.eric.ed.gov/fulltext/EJ1293141.pdf

Pei, M., Wu, Y., & Yang, Y. (2023). Can reflective interventions improve students' academic achievement? A meta-analysis. *Thinking Skills and Creativity, 49,* 101243. https://doi.org/10.1016/j.tsc.2023.101243

Pozas, M., Letzel, V., Linder, KT, Schwab., S. (2021). The effect of differentiated instruction on students' well-being, social inclusion, and academic self-concept in inclusive classrooms. *Frontiers in Education, 6,* https://doi.org/10.3389/feduc.2021.729027

Romero-González, M., Lavigne-Cerván, R., Gamboa-Ternero, S., Rodríguez-Infante, G., Juárez-Ruiz de Mier, R., & Romero-Pérez, J. F. (2023). Active home literacy environment: Parents' and teachers' expectations of its influence on affective relationships at home, reading performance, and reading motivation in children aged 6 to 8 years. *Frontiers in Psychology, 14,* 1261662. https://doi.org/10.3389/fpsyg.2023.1261662

Rutgers NJAES. (n.d.). Learning through the garden. Rutgers New Jersey Agricultural Experiment Station. Retrieved https://njaes.rutgers.edu/fs1211/

Zaur, J. (2021). Aligning goals, objectives, and standards in lesson plans. Education World. Retrieved February 1, 2025, from https://www.educationworld.com/teachers/aligning-goals-objectives-and-standards-lesson-plans

3

G is for Goal-Directed Instruction

> What a child can do with assistance today, she will be able to do by herself tomorrow.
> —Lev Vygotsky, Education Psychologist

Goal-directed instruction is a cornerstone of effective teaching in special education, offering a structured approach tailored to the unique needs and abilities of each student. By focusing on specific, measurable objectives, this method ensures that learning is purposeful and aligned with individual education plans (IEPs). Goal-oriented instruction promotes clarity for both teachers and students, fostering a sense of direction and achievement. It also allows educators to track progress, adjust strategies, and celebrate successes, no matter how small. This approach is particularly valuable in special education, where personalized goals can address academic, social, and functional skills critical for long-term growth and independence.

The Value and Implementation of Goal-Oriented Instruction

Goal-oriented instruction is a vital framework for special education, ensuring that teaching is purposeful, measurable, and aligned with the unique needs of each student. This approach centers on setting specific, achievable goals that guide the educational process, fostering a sense of progress and accomplishment for both students and teachers. In the context of special education, goal-oriented instruction plays a critical role in addressing diverse learning abilities, promoting independence, and equipping students with skills necessary for personal and academic success (Rusbult, 2002). This detailed discussion explores the significance of goal-oriented instruction and provides strategies for its effective implementation.

The Value of Goal-Oriented Instruction

Personalized Learning and Individual Progress (Wilbrecht & Davidow, 2024). In special education, students often have varying abilities, strengths, and challenges. Goal-oriented instruction allows educators to tailor teaching strategies to each student's unique needs by setting IEP goals. These goals focus on specific academic, social, or functional skills, ensuring that instruction is relevant and impactful. This personalized approach provides a clear pathway for progress and helps students achieve milestones at their own pace.

Clarity and Focus (Wilbrecht & Davidow, 2024). Clear, measurable goals give both teachers and students a defined target to work toward. For educators, these goals provide a framework for lesson planning, instructional methods, and assessment. For students, understanding their objectives helps them stay motivated and engaged, fostering a sense of ownership over their learning. This focus minimizes distractions and ensures that all efforts are aligned with meaningful outcomes.

Monitoring and Measuring Progress (O'Rourke & Spencer, 2018; Nedzinskaitė-Mačiūnienė & Šimienė, 2021). Goal-oriented instruction fosters accountability by enabling educators to systematically track student progress and make informed instructional decisions. Regular monitoring ensures students remain on a clear path toward their objectives, while offering timely feedback for both learners and teachers. For example, progress reports can highlight trends in student achievement over time, data collection tools like checklists or digital tracking systems can measure specific skill development, and observational assessments during class activities can reveal how well students are applying what they've learned. By using these varied methods, educators can continuously evaluate what's working, identify areas needing adjustment, and fine-tune their instruction to maximize student growth.

Encouraging Independence and Confidence (Butler, 2019; Hu et al., 2023; Ma, 2021; Moeller et al., 2012). By setting achievable and incrementally challenging goals, students gain confidence as they experience success. This sense of accomplishment motivates them to take on more complex tasks, fostering independence and self-efficacy. For example, a student learning to write their name may progress to writing simple sentences, gradually building their skills and self-belief.

Collaboration and Consistency (Bruhn et al., 2016; Grant, 2012; Rowe et al., 2017; Zimmerman, 2002). The collaborative nature of goal-oriented instruction fosters communication among educators, parents, therapists, and other stakeholders. IEP goals serve as a shared focus, ensuring that everyone involved in a student's education is working toward the same objectives. This consistency across environments reinforces learning and provides a supportive network for the student.

Implementation of Goal-Oriented Instruction

Implementing goal-oriented instruction requires thoughtful planning, collaboration, and flexibility. Below are strategies and best practices for ensuring its success in all classrooms including special education classrooms:

Develop Clear, Measurable Goals (Hedin & DeSpain, 2018). While SMART goals (Specific, Measurable, Achievable, Relevant, Time-bound) are widely used, they're not the only option. There are multiple effective frameworks for crafting clear and meaningful learning objectives—especially when your focus includes flexibility, creativity, or therapeutic outcomes. These alternative approaches can better support diverse learners and instructional goals.

ABC(D) Method: A popular alternative in education and therapy, especially when writing objectives for individualized plans.

- A = Audience—Who is doing the learning?
- B = Behavior—What will the learner do?
- C = Condition—Under what circumstances?
- D = Degree—How well must they do it?

KUD Format (Know–Understand–Do): Great for unit planning or broader learning goals.

- Know—Key facts, vocabulary, or concepts.
- Understand—Big ideas or principles.
- Do—Skills or processes students will apply.

MAGER's Performance-Based Objectives: Similar to ABCD, this focuses on observable and assessable outcomes:

- Performance—What should the student be able to do?
- Conditions—Under what conditions?
- Criterion—How well must it be done?

Bloom's Taxonomy-Based Objectives: Use action verbs from Bloom's levels (Remember, Understand, Apply, Analyze, Evaluate, Create) to guide objectives at different levels of cognitive demand.
Example:

- *Remember:* List the steps of a trick
- *Understand:* Explain why each step is important
- *Apply:* Perform the trick
- *Analyze:* Identify what made the trick successful or not
- *Evaluate:* Give feedback on a peer's performance
- *Create:* Invent a new trick with your own script

Base Goals on Assessment and Observation (Full Sped Ahead, 2023; Lane, 2023). Accurate assessment is essential for setting meaningful and achievable goals. Educators should draw on a variety of tools—including formal and informal assessments, pre-assessments to establish baseline understanding, post-assessments to measure growth, and summative evaluations to gauge overall achievement. Classroom observations, input from parents and specialists, and ongoing formative feedback further enrich this data. Together, these sources provide a comprehensive picture of the student's current abilities and challenges, ensuring that goals are both realistic and personalized to their unique needs.

Break Goals into Manageable Steps (Mcconomy et al., 2022). Long-term goals can feel overwhelming, particularly for students with special needs. Breaking these goals into smaller, manageable steps helps students experience success more often, which builds confidence, maintains motivation, and supports steady skill development. For example, a goal like learning to tie shoelaces can begin with simply forming the initial knot before gradually moving toward completing the entire sequence. Similarly, reading skills are built step by step—starting with letter recognition, then linking letters to sounds, blending those sounds into words, progressing to reading simple sentences, and eventually understanding full paragraphs and multi-page texts. This scaffolded approach ensures that progress is both measurable and meaningful.

Incorporate Student Interests and Strengths (Tadic, 2019). Engaging students in goal-setting and incorporating their interests makes learning more meaningful and enjoyable. For instance, a student interested in animals might work on reading comprehension using stories about wildlife. Leveraging strengths also helps students feel more confident and capable of achieving their objectives.

Use Visual Supports and Tools (Foster-Cohen & Mirfin-Veitch, 2017). Visual aids such as charts, checklists, and progress trackers can help students understand their goals and monitor their achievements. For nonverbal or younger students, pictorial representations of steps or rewards can make goals more accessible and engaging.

Incorporate Flexible Teaching Methods (Hughes, 2024). Students with special needs often require diverse approaches to learning. Goal-oriented instruction allows teachers to use various methods, such as hands-on activities, technology, or group work, to address individual learning styles and challenges. For example, a student struggling with math concepts might benefit from using manipulatives or educational apps.

Involve Families and Caregivers (International Education Studies, 2018; Networks, 2020; U.S. Department of Education, 2021). Parents and caregivers play a critical role in reinforcing goals at home. Regular communication and collaboration ensure consistency across settings. Educators can provide resources and suggestions to help families support their child's progress outside the classroom.

Evaluate and Adjust Goals as Needed (Hughes, 2024). Flexibility is key to goal-oriented instruction. As students' progress, goals may need to be revised to reflect their achievements or address new challenges. Regularly reviewing and updating goals ensures that instruction remains relevant and effective.

Challenges and Solutions

In today's inclusive classrooms, effective teaching requires more than just content knowledge—it demands strategic collaboration, thoughtful goal-setting, and flexible support systems. One teacher's approach demonstrates how intentional teamwork and clear instructional priorities can create a highly supportive learning environment for students with diverse needs.

To manage the complexities of goal-oriented instruction, this educator began by prioritizing the most critical learning goals, focusing on what would have the greatest impact on student development. By narrowing the focus, instruction became more manageable, targeted, and meaningful for students.

Understanding the value of collaboration, the teacher held regular co-planning meetings with paraprofessionals, therapists, and specialists. These sessions, even brief ones, allowed the team to align their strategies and share responsibilities. For example, while the teacher led the main lesson, the occupational therapist embedded fine motor skill development into writing tasks, and the paraprofessional worked with small groups needing reinforcement. This intentional use of support staff ensured that students received comprehensive and consistent assistance throughout the day.

To stay responsive to student needs, the team maintained ongoing communication through quick check-ins and shared digital logs. They also leveraged technology tools such as progress monitoring software and adaptive learning platforms to collect data efficiently and adjust instruction based on real-time feedback. These tools helped track student progress and personalize learning paths effectively.

Consistency across learning environments was another key element. The team used unified language, visual supports, and prompts to create predictable routines for students. During instruction, staff rotated roles, co-facilitated activities, and adjusted grouping to provide differentiated support without interrupting the flow of learning.

When it came to setting and reviewing goals—whether for an IEP or classroom benchmarks—the teacher actively involved all support personnel. Each member contributed unique insights based on their direct experience with the students, ensuring that goals were both realistic and individualized.

By thoughtfully balancing priorities, utilizing support staff, and integrating purposeful technology, this educator created a collaborative, student-centered classroom where every learner had the opportunity to grow and succeed.

Bringing Learning to Life

For several years, I taught a university-level course for pre-service teachers focused on the intersection of the arts and disability. When I first designed the course, it was primarily intended for special education majors. The goal was to introduce students to how the arts are implemented in educational settings—whether as standalone curriculum, through arts-enhanced activities, or using arts-integrated instructional strategies.

In the early iterations of the course, the structure was traditional: quizzes during the first several weeks, academic readings to summarize, and projects to design and implement. I had carefully written learning objectives, created detailed lesson plans, and outlined both formative and summative assessments. On paper, it was a well-organized course.

But then I began my own doctoral program—and it changed the way I looked at teaching. I started asking myself a critical question: *What is the purpose of this assignment?* That question shifted everything. I took a fresh look at the course with new eyes. I refined and clarified the assignments, eliminated ones that didn't serve a clear purpose, and ensured that every task had specific, measurable learning goals—not just for me but for the students as well. And something amazing happened.

My students became more engaged. They submitted their work on time, and their assignments were richer, more thoughtful, and more useful. They understood what they were working toward—and why it mattered. At the end of that semester, student evaluations reflected a noticeable shift. The feedback wasn't just positive—it was detailed. Students articulated what they had learned and how they planned to apply it in their future classrooms.

But perhaps the most surprising change was who began enrolling in the course. It was no longer just special education majors. Students from elementary education, early childhood, art education, art therapy, psychology, and social work—and even business—started signing up. To meet the needs of this diverse group, I individualized project goals by major, helping each student see how the content connected to their field.

This experience reinforced the power of goal-directed instruction. When students know what they're expected to learn—and how they're expected to demonstrate that learning—the process becomes more relevant, exciting, and meaningful. And for me, it was a powerful reminder that when we design with intention and clarity, learning becomes a truly transformative experience.

Summary

Goal-directed instruction is an indispensable strategy in special education, providing structure, clarity, and a pathway for meaningful progress. By setting individualized, measurable goals, educators can address diverse needs, build confidence, and prepare students for future challenges. Effective implementation requires collaboration, creativity, and ongoing assessment, ensuring that instruction remains flexible and tailored to each learner. Through goal-oriented instruction, special education classrooms become empowering spaces where students develop the skills and confidence to achieve their fullest potential.

 **Discussion Questions**

1. How does goal-oriented instruction empower you and your students to develop independence and confidence, and what are some real-world examples you"ve seen or can imagine?
2. What do you think are the advantages and potential challenges of using one of the methods to ensure goals remain both ambitious and achievable?
3. In what ways can incorporating students" interests and strengths into their IEP goals increase motivation and engagement in the classroom?
4. How can you effectively collaborate with families, specialists, and support staff to ensure consistency and success in achieving student goals across different environments?
5. What role does regular assessment and feedback play in the success of goal-oriented instruction?

References

Bruhn, A. L., McDaniel, S. C., Fernando, J., & Troughton, L. (2016). Goal-setting interventions for students with behavior problems: A systematic review. *Behavioral Disorders, 41*(2), 107–121.

Butler, J. A. (2019). *Do goal setting and student-directed learning lead to gains in self-motivation and academic performance?* (Master's thesis). University of Wisconsin-River Falls. Retrieved from https://minds.wisconsin.edu/handle/1793/82435

Foster-Cohen, S., & Mirfin-Veitch, B. (2017). Evidence for the effectiveness of visual supports in helping children with disabilities access the mainstream primary school curriculum. *Journal of Research in Special Educational Needs, 17*(2), 79–86.

Full SPED Ahead. (2023). The importance of progress monitoring and baseline assessments in special education. Full SPED Ahead. Retrieved January 25, 2025, from https://www.fullspedahead.com/progress-monitoring-in-special-education/

Grant, A. M. (2012). An integrated model of goal-focused coaching: An evidence-based framework for teaching and practice. *International Coaching Psychology Review, 7*(2), 146–165.

Hedin, L., & DeSpain, S. (2018). SMART or not? Writing specific, measurable IEP goals. *Teaching Exceptional Children, 51*(2), 100–110.

Hu, Z., Shan, N., & Jiao, R. (2023). The relationships between perceived teacher autonomy support, academic self-efficacy, and learning engagement among primary school students: A network analysis. *European Journal of Psychology of Education*, 1–14. https://doi.org/10.1007/s10212-023-00703-7

Hughes, H. (2024). Flexibility: The key to an inclusive education for special education students in general education classrooms. Retrieved from https://scholarworks.calstate.edu/downloads/w3763g91h

Lane, W. (2023). What are formal and informal assessments in special education? Dr. William Lane, *Special Education*. Retrieved April 27, 2025, from https://www.drwilliamlane.com/blog/what-are-formal-and-informal-assessments-in-special-education

Ma, Q. (2021). The Role of Teacher Autonomy Support on Students' Academic Engagement and Resilience. *Frontier in Psychology, 12*. 778581. https://doi.org/10.3389/fpsyg.2021.778581

McConomy, A., Root, J., & Wade, T. (2022). Using task analysis to support inclusion and assessment in the classroom. *Teaching Exceptional Children*, *54*(6), 366–375. https://files.eric.ed.gov/fulltext/EJ1350324.pdf

Moeller, A. J., Theiler, J. M., & Wu, C. (2012). Goal setting and student achievement: A longitudinal study. *The Modern Language Journal*, *96*(ii), 153–169. https://doi.org/10.1111/j.1540-4781.2011.01231.x

Nedzinskaitė-Mačiūnienė, R., & Šimienė, G. (2021). A strategic and goal-directed student: Expectations vs. reality. In *Improving inclusive education through universal design for learning* (pp. 187–215). Cham: Springer International Publishing.

O'Rourke, S., Spencer, K., & Kelly, F. (2018). Development and psychometric investigation of an arts integrated assessment instrument for educators. *Journal for Learning Through the Arts*, *14*(1), 1–20. https://escholarship.org/uc/item/0mx5z5xd

Rowe, D. A., Mazzotti, V. L., Ingram, A., & Lee, S. (2017). Effects of goal-setting instruction on academic engagement for students at risk. *Career Development and Transition for Exceptional Individuals*, *40*(1), 25–35.

Rusbult, C. (2002). Aesop's activities: Effective teaching strategies for goal-directed education. Retrieved from https://www.asa3.org/ASA/education/teach/aesop.htm

Tadic, N. (2019). 'My brain hurts': Incorporating learner interests into the classroom. *Language and education*, *33*(1), 68–84.

U.S. Department of Education. (2021). Supporting parent and family engagement to enhance students' academic achievement. Retrieved from https://files.eric.ed.gov/fulltext/ED641298.pdf

Wilbrecht, L., & Davidow, J. Y. (2024). Goal-directed learning in adolescence: Neurocognitive development and contextual influences. *Nature Reviews Neuroscience*, *25*(3), 176–194.

Zimmerman, B. J. (2002). Becoming a self-regulated learner: An overview. *Theory Into Practice*, *41*(2), 64–70. https://doi.org/10.1207/s15430421tip4102_2

4

I is for Imaginative Teaching

> Imagination does not become great until human beings, given the courage and strength, use it to create.
> —Maria Montessori, Educator and Innovator

> Imagination is more important than knowledge. Knowledge is limited. Imagination encircles the world.
> —Albert Einstein, Inventor

Imaginative teaching is an approach that emphasizes creativity, innovation, and active engagement in the learning process. It encourages educators to use dynamic, flexible, and often unconventional teaching methods to inspire curiosity, problem-solving, and critical thinking. At times, it requires us to step outside of our comfort zone. This approach goes beyond traditional lecture-based instruction, incorporating techniques like storytelling, role-playing, hands-on activities, visual arts, music, and even movement to make lessons more interactive and meaningful.

For diverse learners, the goal of imaginative teaching is to make learning more engaging and accessible. By appealing to different senses and learning styles, it helps students connect with the material in personal, memorable ways. In the process, students are not just passive recipients of information but active participants in their own learning journey.

Imaginative teaching is particularly effective for fostering creativity, building confidence, and creating an inclusive classroom environment where all students, regardless of ability, feel empowered to explore, experiment, and learn. Ultimately, imaginative teaching transforms learning into a meaningful, stimulating experience that empowers all students, helping them connect with the material and with each other in deeper ways.

The Value and Implementation of Imagination and Imaginative Teaching

Imaginative teaching harnesses the creative potential of both teachers and students to make learning more engaging, accessible, and personalized. By using imaginative approaches, educators can tap into the strengths of students with disabilities, fostering a deeper understanding, emotional connection, and motivation for learning. This detailed exploration discusses the value of imagination and how imaginative teaching strategies can be implemented in the classroom to reach students of all abilities.

The Value of Imagination Teaching

Enhancing Engagement and Motivation (Sodsod, 2025). Imagination fuels engagement by transforming the learning experience into something exciting and dynamic. Students with diverse learning needs, especially those who struggle with traditional learning methods, often benefit from more interactive and creative approaches. Imaginative teaching methods, such as role-playing, storytelling, or visual arts, capture students' attention and spark their curiosity, making lessons more interesting (active learning). This increase in engagement helps combat feelings of frustration or disinterest, leading to improved motivation and participation.

Fostering Creativity and Problem-Solving Skills (Langer, 2012; Ülger, 2016). Imaginative teaching encourages creative thinking, which is crucial for problem-solving and adapting to new challenges. For students with disabilities, imagination can be a powerful means of expression and understanding. By engaging in creative tasks, such as designing projects, creating stories, or imagining scenarios, students develop critical thinking skills and the ability to approach problems from different angles. This process builds confidence and autonomy, allowing students to feel empowered in their learning journey.

Encouraging Emotional Expression and Social Development (Tsortanidou et al., 2022). Imagination allows students to explore their emotions and express themselves in safe, supportive ways. In the special education classroom, imaginative activities like role-playing, drama, or art provide students with the opportunity to work through emotions, practice empathy, and understand the perspectives of others. These activities contribute to social and emotional development by building interpersonal skills, self-regulation, and emotional intelligence, all of which are essential for functioning in everyday life.

Differentiating Instruction (Egan, 2005; Nielsen, 2006; Tomlinson, 2014). One of the core challenges in teaching diverse learners is catering to the needs and abilities of students. Imaginative teaching provides flexibility in lesson delivery, allowing teachers to adjust activities to suit a wide range of learning styles and abilities. For example, while one student may learn best through visual storytelling, another might benefit from kinesthetic learning through physical activities. Imagination empowers teachers to create adaptive learning experiences that are accessible and engaging for all students.

Building Confidence and Self-Esteem (Akpan & Beard, 2016). Imaginative teaching often includes hands-on, experiential learning that allows students to see tangible results from their efforts. Completing a creative project, acting out a scene, or solving a problem through imagination provides students with a sense of accomplishment and pride in their work. These activities reinforce positive self-esteem, helping students recognize their capabilities and value as learners. As students experience success in imaginative tasks, they are more likely to take risks and engage with new challenges, fostering resilience and perseverance.

Promoting Collaboration and Communication (Cremin et al., 2006; Egan, 2005). Imaginative teaching frequently involves collaborative activities, such as group projects, cooperative games, or shared storytelling. Working together on imaginative tasks encourages students to communicate, share ideas, and support each other. These collaborative experiences not only enhance academic learning but also build critical social skills such as teamwork, negotiation, and conflict resolution. For students with communication challenges, these activities provide a structured environment to practice social interaction in a low-pressure setting.

Implementation of Imaginative Teaching

To effectively implement imaginative teaching, educators must be thoughtful and intentional in their approach. Here are several strategies and considerations for incorporating imagination into instruction:

Use Multisensory Approaches (Abdulla & Eissa, 2019; Maliki & Yasin, 2017). Imaginative teaching thrives when it engages multiple senses. For students with disabilities, multisensory learning experiences make abstract concepts more concrete. For example, using tactile materials, like textured letters for reading, or incorporating music and sound effects in storytelling, can help students with sensory processing issues better engage with content. By appealing to visual, auditory, and kinesthetic senses, imaginative activities increase the likelihood of reaching diverse learners and enhancing understanding.

Incorporate Storytelling and Drama (Dunsmuir & Wright, 2019; Ehsan, 2017; Stubbs & Sorenson, 2025; Thompson & Johnson, 2013). Storytelling is a powerful tool in the special education classroom, allowing students to explore new ideas, express emotions, and develop language skills. Teachers can use storytelling to introduce new concepts, create engaging narratives around subjects, or allow students to develop their own stories. Drama and role-playing activities can help students practice social situations, problem-solving, and empathy. By stepping into different roles or acting out scenarios, students gain a deeper understanding of themselves and others, building both cognitive and social skills.

Integrate Art and Music (Deasy, 2020; Evans, 2024). Art and music are particularly effective forms of imaginative teaching for students with special needs. Artistic activities such as painting, drawing, sculpting, or collage-making offer students a chance to express ideas and emotions visually. Similarly, music, whether through listening or active participation (e.g., singing, playing instruments), engages students' creativity and promotes emotional expression. Art and music can be used to explore various themes, reinforce academic content, or simply provide an outlet for personal expression.

Incorporate Play-Based Learning (Alordiah, 2023; Taylor & Boyer, 2020). Play is a natural, enjoyable form of learning that encourages imagination and creativity. In the special education classroom, play-based learning can take many forms, including building with blocks, role-playing with dolls or puppets, or engaging in cooperative games. These activities not only enhance cognitive development but also provide opportunities for socialization, problem-solving, and emotional expression. Play-based learning helps students engage in low-stress, high-reward activities that foster critical thinking and interpersonal skills.

Personalize Learning with Student Interests (Alamri et al., 2024; Solari et al., 2022). To maximize the value of imaginative teaching, educators should consider students' personal interests and incorporate them into the learning process. Whether a student is passionate about animals, outer space, or art, teachers can design imaginative lessons that align with those interests, making learning more relevant and enjoyable. Personalized learning experiences allow students to see the connection between their passions and educational content, which in turn increases motivation and enthusiasm.

Create a Safe, Supportive Environment (Henriksen et al., 2020; Sawyer, 2021). Imaginative teaching requires a classroom atmosphere that encourages creativity, risk-taking, and exploration. Teachers should foster a supportive, non-judgmental environment where students feel comfortable expressing themselves and experimenting with new ideas. Providing positive reinforcement, celebrating effort over perfection, and emphasizing the value of trying new things all contribute to an environment where imagination can thrive.

Incorporate Technology (Di Blas, 2022; Lin et al., 2024). Technology can be a powerful tool for imaginative teaching. Interactive apps, virtual reality, and digital storytelling platforms can all enhance students' creativity and engagement. For example, students could create digital stories, use apps to build virtual environments, or explore imaginative worlds through virtual reality. Technology provides unique, accessible opportunities for students to explore their imagination while reinforcing educational concepts.

Challenges and Solutions

While imaginative teaching offers numerous benefits, it may come with challenges, such as limited resources, the need for specialized training, or the challenge of maintaining structure in creative activities. To address these challenges:

- **Resourcefulness:** Teachers can be resourceful by using inexpensive or everyday materials for creative activities (e.g., recycled materials for art projects).
- **Training:** Professional development and workshops on creative strategies can help educators feel confident in implementing imaginative teaching techniques.
- **Balancing Structure:** While creativity is essential, maintaining a balance with structure ensures that imaginative activities are purposeful and aligned with learning objectives.

Bringing Learning to Life

We often ask our students to stretch their imaginations—to take risks, step outside their comfort zones, and embrace creative thinking as part of their learning journey. But I've led enough professional development sessions to know that when we ask adults, especially educators, to do the same, the response is often hesitation—or even a little embarrassment. Sound familiar?

So I'm inviting you to do just that. To imagine. To take a creative leap. To consider what it looks like when we model imaginative, out-of-the-box thinking for our students.

I was once asked to design a unit on the Solar System for a group of fifth graders. The goal? Fully engage their imaginations while meeting the science standards. I decided to take an arts-integrated approach—one that would align core science content with standards from music, visual arts, dance, and theater. I also collaborated with the school's arts educators to bring the lessons to life.

We began with music, working alongside the music teacher to introduce students to Gustav Holst's orchestral suite, *The Planets, Op. 32*. As they listened to each movement, students used their imaginations to connect the sounds and moods of the music to the characteristics of each planet.

We also had an important conversation: Why weren't Earth and Pluto included in Holst's suite? The answer sparked curiosity—Holst was inspired by astrology, not astronomy, and in astrology, Earth holds no significance because it's the observational point. And Pluto? It hadn't even been discovered yet.

In visual art, we explored the work of Alexander Calder, whose kinetic sculptures—mobiles—revolutionized traditional sculpture by adding movement and whimsy. Inspired by his work, students created their own solar system mobiles, reinforcing both artistic and scientific principles.

Through dance, we explored movement concepts like rotation and revolution. Each student embodied a planet, taking their place in orbit around a "sun" at the center. As they physically moved through space, they deepened their understanding of celestial motion through embodied learning.

With the drama teacher, we turned to reader's theater. Students rehearsed and performed *The Milky Way's Got Talent* by Kathy Applebee—a playful, theatrical way to reinforce what they had learned while developing their fluency and expression.

To culminate the unit, students brought it all together in a performance called *The Dance of the Solar System,* presented to the second graders. It was joyful, imaginative teaching in action—where content knowledge and creative expression met seamlessly, and students were fully engaged, body and mind.

This unit reminded me that when we, as educators, embrace creativity ourselves, we give students permission to do the same. And in that space, learning becomes meaningful, memorable, and magical.

Summary

Imaginative teaching is an invaluable tool in the special education classroom, enriching the learning experience by engaging students in creative and interactive ways. By incorporating imagination into instruction, teachers can meet the diverse needs of students, fostering a love for learning, boosting confidence, and promoting social and emotional development. With thoughtful planning and an openness to creativity, educators can transform their classrooms into spaces where imagination leads to academic success and personal growth for all students.

Discussion Questions

1. In what ways can you incorporate imaginative teaching methods, like storytelling or role-playing, to enhance engagement and emotional expression for your students?
2. How can you balance creativity and structure in imaginative lessons to ensure learning objectives are still being met?
3. What are some strategies you can use to incorporate students' personal interests into imaginative activities, and why is this important for diverse learners?
4. How might multisensory and play-based approaches support diverse learning styles? Can you give examples from your own experience?
5. What are some of the challenges you may face when implementing imaginative teaching, and how can you overcome them with limited resources or training?

References

Abdulla, M. A., & Eissa, M. A. (2019). Investigating the effect of multisensory approach on improving emergent literacy skills in children with autism spectrum disorder. *Topics in Early Childhood Special Education, 34*(3), 142–153.

Alamri, H., Alzahrani, A., & Alzahrani, S. (2024). The impact of personalized learning on intrinsic motivation, academic proficiency, and behavioral issues in the classroom. ERIC. https://eric.ed.gov/?ff1=dtyIn_2024&id=ED651862&q=personalized+learning

Alordiah, C. (2023). Understanding the role of play in promoting cognitive, social, and emotional development in school children: Implications for counselors and evaluators. ResearchGate. https://www.researchgate.net/profile/Caroline-Alordiah/publication/374419878_UNDERSTANDING_THE_ROLE_OF_PLAY_IN_PROMOTING_COGNITIVE_SOCIAL_AND_EMOTIONAL_DEVELOPMENT_IN_SCHOOL_CHILDREN_IMPLICATIONS_FOR_COUNSELLORS_AND_EVALUATORS/links/651d2073b0df2f20a20e928c/UNDERSTANDING-THE-ROLE-OF-PLAY-IN-PROMOTING-COGNITIVE-SOCIAL-AND-EMOTIONAL-DEVELOPMENT-IN-SCHOOL-CHILDREN-IMPLICATIONS-FOR-COUNSELLORS-AND-EVALUATORS.pdf

Akpan, J. P., & Beard, L. A. (2016). Using constructivist teaching strategies to enhance academic outcomes of students with special needs. *Universal Journal of Educational Research, 4*(2), 392–398. https://doi.org/10.13189/ujer.2016.040211

Cremin, T., Burnard, P., & Craft, A. (2006). Pedagogy and possibility thinking in the early years. *Thinking Skills and Creativity, 1*(2), 108–119. https://doi.org/10.1016/j.tsc.2006.07.001

Deasy, R. (2020). Critical links: Learning in the arts and student academic and social development. Arts Education Partnership. Retrieved April 27, 2025, from https://www.aep-arts.org/wp-content/uploads/Critical-Links_-Learning-in-the-Arts-and-Student-Academic-and-Social-Development.pdf

Di Blas, N. (2022). Authentic learning, creativity, and collaborative digital storytelling: Lessons from a large-scale case study. *Educational Technology & Society, 25*(2), 80–104.

Dunsmuir, S., & Wright, D. (2019). The effectiveness of storytelling interventions in supporting language development in children. *Journal of Child Development Studies, University College London*, 1 –20. https://discovery.ucl.ac.uk/id/eprint/10066448/1/Dunsmuir_Wright%20%20Dunsmuir%20%282019%29%20-%20final%20accepted.pdf

Egan, K. (2005). *An imaginative approach to teaching*. Jossey-Bass.

Ehsan, S. (2017). The impact of storytelling on children's intellectual and social development. *Procedia - Social and Behavioral Sciences*, *187*, 91–98. https://doi.org/10.1016/j.sbspro.2015.03.172

Evans, M. (2024). Does art education matter in inclusiveness for learners with disabilities? *International Journal of Learning, Teaching and Educational Research*, *23*(10), 1–15. https://doi.org/10.26803/ijlter.23.10.1

Henriksen, D., Creely, E., & Henderson, M. (2020). Creativity and risk-taking in teaching and learning settings: Insights from six international narratives. *Creativity Studies*, *13*(1), 1–16. https://doi.org/10.3846/cs.2020.11027

Langer, J. A. (2012). The interplay of creative and critical thinking in instruction. In *Design research on learning and thinking in educational settings* (pp. 65–82). Routledge.

Lin, X. P., Li, B. B., Yao, Z. N., Yang, Z., & Zhang, M. (2024). The impact of virtual reality on student engagement in the classroom: A critical review of the literature. *Frontiers in Psychology*, *15*, 1360574. https://doi.org/10.3389/fpsyg.2024.1360574

Maliki, N. S. M., & Yasin, M. H. M. (2017). Application of multisensory in learning alphabets identification skills for special education students. *Journal of ICSAR*, *1*(2), 150–155.

Nielsen, T. W. (2006). Towards a pedagogy of imagination: A phenomenological case study of holistic education. *Ethnography and Education*, *1*(2), 247–264. https://doi.org/10.1080/17457820600715455

Sawyer, R. K. (2021). The dialogue of creativity: Teaching the creative process by animating student work as a collaborating creative agent. *Cognition and Instruction*, *40*(4), 459–487. https://doi.org/10.1080/07370008.2021.1958219

Sodsod, A. B. (2025). Teachers' creative teaching strategies, learners' motivation to learn, and learning engagement among children with special needs in selected schools in cavite. *Journal of Education and Liberal Studies, 2*(1), 1–1.

Solari, M., Vizquerra, M. I., & Engel, A. (2022). Students' interests for personalized learning: An analysis guide. *European Journal of Psychology of Education, 38*(5), 1073–1109. https://doi.org/10.1007/s10212-022-00656-3

Stubbs, R., & Sorensen, N. (2025). Tabletop role-playing games and social and emotional learning in school settings. *Social and Emotional Learning: Research, Practice, and Policy, 5*, Article 100090. https://doi.org/10.1016/j.sel.2025.100090

Taylor, M., & Boyer, E. (2020). Play-based learning: Playing the way to rich learning experiences. ERIC. https://files.eric.ed.gov/fulltext/EJ1398486.pdf

Thompson, R. M., & Johnston, S. (2013). Use of social stories to improve self-regulation in children with autism spectrum disorders. *Physical & Occupational Therapy in Pediatrics, 33*(3), 271–284. https://doi.org/10.3109/01942638.2013.768322

Tomlinson, C. A. (2014). *The differentiated classroom: Responding to the needs of all learners* (2nd ed.). ASCD.

Tsortanidou, X., Daradoumis, T., & Barberá, E. (2022). Developing social-emotional skills through imaginative teaching methods in elementary education. *Early Child Development and Care, 192*(8), 1201–1216.

Ülger, K. A. N. İ. (2016). The relationship between creative thinking and critical thinking skills of students. *Hacettepe Universitesi Egitim Fakultesi Dergisi-Hacettepe University Journal of Education, 31*, 695–671.

5

C is for Creativity and Curiosity

Creativity is the process of having original ideas that have value. It is not the same as innate talent. It is a skill that can be developed.
—Sir Kenneth Robinson, Education Expert

It is the supreme art of the teacher to awaken joy in creative expression and knowledge.
—Albert Einstein

True teaching is the art of awakening the natural curiosity of young minds. Parents, teachers, and mentors have the opportunity to enhance skills and foster innovative thinking in children with disabilities by nurturing their inherent curiosity. This approach can positively influence two critical executive functions: cognitive flexibility and cognitive self-control. However, schools often fail to cultivate an environment where students embrace uncertainty and are encouraged to seek answers independently.

Curiosity should be at the heart of education, with each day presenting students with novel experiences that provoke thoughtful inquiry. By allowing children to learn creatively, we alleviate the pressure to always be "right"—a stressor amplified by standardized testing—and empower students to take risks and learn from their mistakes. Through this process, they develop essential skills such as resilience, flexibility, adaptability, critical thinking, and problem-solving. In today's inclusive classrooms, it is imperative to support all students in cultivating the ability and motivation to think beyond conventional boundaries, explore alternative solutions, and navigate unfamiliar situations.

Research from the University of California, Davis, released in Fall 2014, found that individuals who are highly curious about a topic are better equipped to learn that information (Gruber et al., 2014). Similarly, an article in the March 2016 issue of *Scientific American Mind* suggests that children absorb certain content more effectively when it is presented through elements of magic and imagination. These findings underscore the role curiosity plays in triggering motivation, a key factor in academic success.

Additionally, studies conducted by the University of Michigan (Shah et al., 2018) have shown that students who explore the relationship between curiosity and creativity tend to achieve higher academic performance. Providing students with stimulating classroom activities that introduce novelty, surprise, and complexity fosters the development of new neural connections, thereby enhancing information retention. Unfortunately, current educational practices often fail to cultivate a sense of inquiry in students. Rather than encouraging students to question and search for answers, traditional methods focus on content delivery that students memorize but rarely internalize.

By reconsidering traditional approaches and allowing ourselves to move beyond conventional methods, we open up new possibilities for fostering deeper learning and critical thinking in students.

Benefits for Diverse Learners

Creativity and curiosity are especially powerful in supporting students with diverse learning needs, including those with disabilities. Traditional teaching methods can often overlook these students' unique strengths, but imaginative and flexible approaches create space for all learners to thrive. When educators nurture curiosity, they encourage students to ask questions, explore interests, and engage more deeply with content—fostering intrinsic motivation and persistence.

Creative activities—such as storytelling, visual arts, music, role-play, and collaborative problem-solving—offer multiple pathways for expression and understanding. These approaches are especially valuable for students who struggle with conventional communication or emotional regulation, allowing them to express feelings, practice empathy, and build social skills in nonverbal or imaginative ways.

Moreover, when students succeed in creative tasks, they build confidence, resilience, and a sense of ownership over their learning. This bolsters self-esteem and reinforces a growth mindset—the belief that effort leads to improvement. In inclusive classrooms, integrating curiosity and creativity not only supports academic growth but also helps learners navigate challenges, connect socially, and develop essential life skills.

The Value and Implementation of Creativity and Curiosity Teaching

Creativity and curiosity are essential components of the learning process, and your diverse learners may face various cognitive, emotional, or physical challenges. Encouraging creativity and nurturing curiosity in the special education classroom are vital for creating an engaging, inclusive, and dynamic environment that caters to the diverse learning needs of students with disabilities. By harnessing these attributes, educators can foster an atmosphere where students feel empowered to explore, experiment, and thrive academically and socially. This chapter explores the value of creativity and curiosity in the special education classroom and provides strategies for effectively implementing these teaching methods.

The Value of Creativity and Curiosity

Enhancing Engagement and Motivation (Beghetto, 2013; Engel, 2011). Curiosity and creativity significantly enhance student engagement. Both are key drivers of intrinsic motivation, leading students to explore, question, and connect with content more deeply. When teaching fosters curiosity and creativity, students are more likely to feel emotionally and cognitively invested in their learning. For students with disabilities, traditional teaching methods can often fail to capture their attention or spark their interest. Creative teaching strategies, such as using art, storytelling, music, or hands-on activities, provide students with novel and engaging ways to interact with the content. Creativity in the classroom breaks away from the rigidity of conventional learning, allowing students to connect with the material on a deeper level. As a result, students are more likely to stay engaged, motivated, and excited about learning. When curiosity is nurtured, it encourages students to ask questions, explore topics of interest, and seek answers, thus fostering intrinsic motivation to learn.

Promoting Critical Thinking and Problem-Solving Skills (Kashdan & Steger, 2007; Kaufman, 2017)). Creativity and curiosity encourage students to think outside the box, explore new ideas, and approach problems from different perspectives. In special education, where students may face unique learning challenges, these skills are particularly important. Encouraging students to experiment with different solutions or brainstorm ideas allows them to develop cognitive flexibility, which is the ability to adapt to changing circumstances or challenges. Creative activities that require problem-solving, such as puzzles, group discussions, or designing projects, help students practice critical thinking and learn how to overcome obstacles in a supportive, safe environment. These skills are transferable to real-life situations, helping students build the confidence to navigate challenges beyond the classroom.

Fostering Emotional Expression and Social Skills (Eisner, 2002; Kashdan & Silvia, 2009; Russ, 2014). Both creativity and curiosity encourage students to explore and articulate their feelings, understand others' perspectives, and engage in meaningful social interactions. They provide an outlet for students to express themselves in ways that go beyond traditional verbal communication. In special education, students with communication challenges, social anxiety, or emotional regulation difficulties may struggle to express their thoughts and feelings. Creative activities, such as drawing, acting, or using role-play, give these students the opportunity to communicate in alternative forms. Through these methods, students can explore their emotions, practice empathy, and build social skills. Imaginative play, for instance, encourages students to step into different roles, helping them develop a greater understanding of social interactions and perspectives. These experiences foster emotional intelligence and social development, both of which are crucial for forming relationships and functioning in society.

Building Confidence and Self-Esteem (Beghetto, 2007; Kashdan & Fincham, 2004). Curiosity and creativity are closely linked to building student confidence and self-esteem. When students are encouraged to explore, take intellectual risks, and express themselves creatively, they develop a stronger sense of identity, competence, and ownership over their learning. These positive experiences directly support confidence and self-esteem. For many students with disabilities, school can be a place of frustration and low self-esteem, particularly if they consistently struggle to meet academic expectations. Creativity offers students opportunities for success in areas where traditional methods may not have worked. Completing an art project, acting in a play, or successfully solving a creative problem can instill a sense of pride and accomplishment. These successes help build confidence and foster a growth mindset—the belief that abilities can improve through effort and persistence. When students feel confident in their abilities, they are more likely to take risks, make mistakes, and persevere in the face of challenges, which are all important aspects of learning and personal growth.

Implementing Creativity and Curiosity

To successfully integrate creativity and curiosity into the special education classroom, educators must be intentional in their approach. Below are several strategies for effectively implementing these elements:

Incorporating Hands-On Learning Activities (Abdelghani et al., 2024; Sinha et al., 2022). One of the most effective ways to engage students is through hands-on learning. Creative activities like building models, conducting experiments, or crafting visual representations of concepts help students engage physically and intellectually. For example, science lessons can involve students in building simple machines or creating dioramas of ecosystems. These types of activities allow students to apply what they've learned in a tangible, meaningful way. Hands-on activities also provide opportunities for students to explore and make mistakes, further developing their problem-solving and critical thinking abilities.

Encouraging Inquiry-Based Learning (Feyzioğlu & Demirci, 2021; Sam, 2024). Curiosity thrives in environments where students are encouraged to ask questions and explore ideas. Inquiry-based learning allows students to explore topics of interest at their own pace, encouraging them to develop a deeper understanding of the material. Teachers can promote inquiry by posing open-ended questions, creating projects that require research, or allowing students to choose topics that spark their curiosity. This approach fosters independent thinking, giving students ownership of their learning while supporting their natural curiosity.

Using Arts and Creative Expression (Corbisiero-Drakos et al, 2021; Eisner, 2002; Wan, 2019). Art, music, drama, and other forms of creative expression are powerful tools for engaging students in the learning process. These activities allow students of all abilities to express themselves in unique and meaningful ways while also developing important skills such as focus, patience, and collaboration. If the arts feel outside your comfort zone, this is an ideal moment to partner with the art professionals in your school or district—they can bring valuable expertise and help bring your ideas to life. For example, students can create visual representations of historical events, write and perform their own plays to demonstrate understanding, or explore musical rhythms to reinforce math concepts. By integrating the arts into lessons, teachers can make learning more accessible, especially for students with disabilities, as these activities offer alternative methods for demonstrating understanding and creativity.

Creating a Safe and Supportive Environment for Exploration (Henriksen et al., 2020; Sawyer, 2021. For many of our students, especially those with disabilities, feeling safe and supported in the classroom is essential for fostering creativity and curiosity. Teachers should establish an inclusive environment where students feel encouraged to take risks and make mistakes without fear of judgment. This includes celebrating effort over perfection and providing positive reinforcement for creativity and innovation. Students should feel that it is acceptable to ask questions, explore new ideas, and experiment with different approaches to solving problems. When students are encouraged to be curious and creative, they are more likely to engage fully in the learning process.

Integrating Technology to Enhance Creativity (Di Blas, 2022; Lin & Chen, 2024). Technology can be a powerful tool for promoting creativity and curiosity in the classroom. Digital platforms, interactive apps, and educational games provide students with opportunities to explore new ideas, collaborate with peers, and engage in creative projects. For example, students can use digital storytelling tools to create multimedia presentations, engage in virtual field trips to explore new environments, or collaborate on interactive projects using educational apps. Technology not only supports creative expression but also makes learning more accessible for students with a range of abilities.

Bringing Learning to Life

At one point in my teaching career, I had a fifth-grade student who unexpectedly began struggling to speak. He didn't stutter, and there was no known medical cause. In fact, up until that point, he had thrived in school—earning straight As, showing kindness, and consistently demonstrating curiosity and intelligence.

The shift happened during his fourth-grade year, after he placed immense pressure on himself to perform well on the National Assessment of Educational Progress (NAEP) test. That pressure became so overwhelming that he lost his ability to speak in certain contexts. (We could have an entire conversation about the impact of standardized testing, but that's a discussion for another time!) After speaking with his parents, I learned he had just begun working with a speech therapist. I asked about strategies they were using and looked for ways to meaningfully integrate those approaches into my classroom—not just for him but to benefit all students.

I've always believed in the power of engaging classroom experiences that go beyond rote learning. I wanted my students to find mastery through process, creativity, and revision—not through the pressure of getting every answer "right." My hope was that by removing the stress of traditional testing, this student—and others—might feel safer to engage, take risks, and grow.

I designed a project that invited students to choose an art discipline and integrate it with academic content they found challenging, blending learning with creative expression and presentation. Students worked in pairs to tackle a complex, open-ended problem of their choosing and develop multiple possible solutions. The task required curiosity, imagination, and collaboration. Most importantly, it allowed space for different forms of expression.

As the project progressed, I noticed something remarkable. During discussions with his partner, the student began tapping his foot lightly—establishing a rhythm. Then, gradually, he began to speak, timing his words with the beat he was setting. By the end of the week-long project, he had gained confidence—not just in his understanding of the content but in his ability to communicate and share ideas.

When it came time for him and his partner to present, he stepped to the front of the class, gently tapped his foot to set the rhythm, and spoke clearly and confidently. His creativity and curiosity had unlocked a path for him to express himself—one that felt safe, empowering, and authentic.

This experience reaffirmed for me the power of creativity and curiosity in the classroom. They don't just support academic learning—they open doors to emotional expression, social connection, and self-confidence. When we provide students with opportunities to explore, create, and collaborate, we offer them new ways to find their voice.

Summary

Creativity and curiosity are invaluable assets in the special education classroom, enabling students to engage deeply with the learning process, develop essential skills, and build confidence in their abilities. By incorporating creative teaching strategies and nurturing curiosity, educators can provide students with disabilities the opportunity to thrive academically, socially, and emotionally. By fostering a classroom environment that values exploration, creativity, and risk-taking, teachers can inspire students to become independent thinkers, problem-solvers, and lifelong learners.

 **Discussion Questions**

1. How can you shift away from a culture of "right answers" to one that values curiosity and the learning process itself, particularly for students with disabilities?
2. In what ways can creative teaching approaches, such as integrating art, music, or hands-on activities, help students build cognitive flexibility and self-control? Can you think of examples from your own experience?
3. How might incorporating students' personal interests into inquiry-based or imaginative learning activities impact their motivation and confidence in the classroom?
4. What are some barriers that you may face when trying to foster curiosity and creativity in inclusive settings, and how can those challenges be addressed realistically?
5. Considering the connection between curiosity, dopamine, and learning (as highlighted by Gruber et al., 2014), how can educators design lessons that naturally trigger curiosity and emotional engagement?

References

Abdelghani, R., Law, E., Desvaux, C., Oudeyer, P.-Y., & Sauzéon, H. (2024). Interactive environments for training children's curiosity through the practice of metacognitive skills: A pilot study. *arXiv preprint arXiv:2403.08397*. https://arxiv.org/abs/2403.08397

Beghetto, R. A. (2007). Creativity research and the classroom: From pitfalls to potential. *Creativity Research Journal, 19*(2–3), 191–206. https://doi.org/10.1142/9789812770868_0006

Beghetto, R. A. (2013). *Killing ideas softly? The promise and perils of creativity in the classroom*. Information Age Publishing.

Corbisiero-Drakos, L., Reeder, L. K., Ricciardi, L., Zacharia, J., & Harnett, S. (2021). Arts integration and 21st century skills: A study of learners and teachers. *International Journal of Education & the Arts, 22*(2). https://eric.ed.gov/?id=EJ1289817

Di Blas, N. (2022). Authentic learning, creativity and collaborative digital storytelling: Lessons from a large-scale case-study. *Educational Technology & Society, 25*(2), 80–104. https://re.public.polimi.it/retrieve/handle/11311/1212476/732303/2022_diblas_ETS.pdf

Eisner, E. W. (2002). *The arts and the creation of mind*. Yale University Press.

Engel, S. (2011). Children's need to know: Curiosity in schools. *Harvard Educational Review, 81*(4), 625–645. https://doi.org/10.17763/haer.81.4.h054131316473115

Feyzioğlu, E. Y., & Demirci, N. (2021). The effects of inquiry-based learning on students' learner autonomy and conceptions of learning. *Journal of Turkish Science Education, 18*(3), 401–420. https://doi.org/10.36681/tused.2021.81

Gruber, M. J., Gelman, B. D., & Ranganath, C. (2014, October 22). States of curiosity modulate hippocampus-dependent learning via the dopaminergic circuit. *Neuron, 84*(2), 486–96. https://doi.org/10.1016/j.neuron.2014.08.060.

Henriksen, K., Stambulova, N., & Roessler, K. K. (2020). Creating the conditions for psychological safety and its impact on athlete development. *International Journal of Sport and Exercise Psychology, 18*(4), 1–19. https://doi.org/10.1016/j.psychsport.2019.101637

Kashdan, T. B., & Fincham, F. D. (2004). Facilitating curiosity: A social and self-regulatory perspective for scientifically based interventions. In P. A. Linley & S. Joseph (Eds.), *Positive Psychology in Practice*, 482–503. John Wiley & Sons.

Kashdan, T. B., & Silvia, P. J. (2009). Curiosity and interest: The benefits of thriving on novelty and challenge. In *Oxford handbook of positive psychology* (2nd ed., pp. 367–374). Oxford University Press.

Kashdan, T. B., & Steger, M. F. (2007). Curiosity and pathways to well-being and meaning in life: Traits, states, and everyday behaviors. *Motivation and Emotion, 31*(3), 159–173. https://doi.org/10.1007/s11031-007-9076-7

Kaufman, S. B. (2017). Curiosity is a unique market of academic success. *The Atlantic,* July 24, 2017.

Lin, H., Chen, Q. (2024). Artificial intelligence (AI) -integrated educational applications and college students' creativity and academic emotions: students and teachers' perceptions and attitudes. *BMC Psychol, 12*(1), 1–12. https://doi.org/10.1186/s40359-024-01979-0

Russ, S. W. (2014). *Pretend play in childhood: Foundation of adult creativity.* American Psychological Association.

Sam, R. (2024). Systematic review of inquiry-based learning: Assessing impact and best practices in education. *F1000Research, 13*, 1045. https://doi.org/10.12688/f1000research.155367.1

Sawyer, R. K. (2021). The dialogue of creativity: Teaching the creative process by animating student work as a collaborating creative agent. *Cognition and Instruction, 40*(4), 459–487. https://doi.org/10.1080/07370008.2021.1958219

Shah, P. E., Weeks, H. M., Richards, B., & Kaciroti, N. (2018). Early childhood curiosity and kindergarten reading and math academic achievement. *Pediatric Research, 84*, 380–386. https://doi.org/10.1038/s41390-018-0039-3

Sinha, T., Bai, Z., & Cassell, J. (2022). A novel multimodal approach for studying the dynamics of curiosity in small group learning. *arXiv preprint arXiv:2204.00545.* https://arxiv.org/abs/2204.00545

Wan, Y. (2019). The role of arts integration and education in improving student outcomes. *Journal of Education and Practice, 10*(4), 1–10. https://files.eric.ed.gov/fulltext/EJ1241600.pdf

6

I is for Immersion

> The student is infinitely more important than the subject matter.
> —Nel Noddings (Ethicist & Education Theorist)

In the next three chapters, we're shifting our focus. While the first five elements—represented by **MAGIC**—have centered on teaching strategies and instructional methods, the final three—**IAN**—will turn inward, focusing on you. These chapters highlight essential behaviors and habits that can enhance your presence, impact, and overall effectiveness in the classroom. And these are developed through a *conscious and deliberate decision* on your part. It's about intentionally strengthening yourself as an educator so you can show up fully and bring your best to your students every single day.

Let's talk about immersion. To effectively engage students, it is essential to be fully immersed in the moment. Being immersed with your students means engaging deeply in their learning experiences—emotionally, intellectually, and relationally. This approach is especially valuable to reach diverse learners where trust, personalization, and responsiveness are essential. Immersive teaching fosters meaningful connections, builds student confidence, and helps create an inclusive environment where all learners feel seen, heard, and supported (Pianta, 1999). Immersion also fosters a safe and stable learning environment. This is particularly important as, in today's classrooms, more than half of students have likely experienced at least three adverse childhood experiences (ACEs) including the global Covid-19 pandemic. Trauma can significantly impact learning, disrupting brain development and affecting memory, mood, relationships, and executive functioning (Burke Harris, 2018; Craig, 2016; Overstreet & Chafouleas, 2016).

When a teacher is genuinely present, students can sense this connection. A teacher who is fully immersed exudes a unique intensity that has a profound effect on the classroom, regardless of the activity. This level of engagement is a powerful tool that positively impacts learning and student relationships. On the other hand, students can easily detect when a teacher is distracted or divided in their attention. A lack of immersion communicates, whether consciously or not, that the moment is not significant enough to warrant undivided focus, which can undermine the learning experience.

For students with disabilities, who may face unique challenges in communication, behavior, or learning, having a teacher who is genuinely present can make a significant difference in their engagement and overall educational experience. When teachers are fully immersed in the moment, they not only model the importance of focus and connection but also cultivate an atmosphere where students feel empowered to explore, ask questions, and take risks in their learning. This level of presence fosters emotional security, encourages meaningful interactions, and strengthens the teacher-student relationship, all of which are crucial for fostering academic and social growth in special education (Jennings & Greenberg, 2009; Tomlinson, 2014).

The Value and Implementation of Being Fully Immersed

In effective learning environments, teaching extends beyond delivering content—it requires educators to be immersed in the instructional process and immersed (fully present) with their students. Immersion means actively engaging with the flow of teaching while offering undivided attention, emotional attunement, and genuine connection. Together, these qualities create a classroom atmosphere built on trust, emotional safety, and responsiveness. This approach is especially powerful in special education settings, where students may encounter challenges in cognitive, emotional, or social development. When teachers are deeply engaged and emotionally available, they foster stronger relationships, encourage risk-taking in learning, and support meaningful growth in both academic and personal development.

The Value of Being Fully Immersed

Building Trust and Emotional Safety (Allen et al., 2018; Mitchell et al., 2018). Our diverse learners often experience heightened levels of anxiety or insecurity due to their struggles with communication, socialization, or behavior. This may be true for many of the students in our classrooms. Being fully immersed in the classroom allows educators to create a trusting and emotionally safe environment, essential for students to feel comfortable engaging in learning activities. Trust is foundational in education; students are more likely to step outside their comfort zone, take risks, ask questions, and express themselves when they feel their teacher is genuinely invested in their success. Emotional safety also enables students to work through challenges without fear of judgment, promoting a growth mindset where effort is valued over perfection.

Enhancing Student Engagement (Pedler et al., 2020; Wentzel, 2010). Immersion increases the teacher's capacity to connect with students, making learning more relevant and engaging. When educators are wholly present, they can better respond to the needs and interests of their students, adjusting their teaching methods in real time. This level of attentiveness helps prevent disengagement, as students can sense when an instructor is actively involved in the lesson. In special education, where students often need tailored instruction and individualized attention, this immersion becomes even more crucial. Teachers who are fully immersed in the classroom can adjust lessons on the fly, offer immediate support, and keep students focused on the task at hand. This engagement leads to higher levels of participation and, ultimately, better learning outcomes.

Modeling Emotional and Behavioral Regulation (Darling-Hammond et al., 2019; Schonert-Reichl, 2017). For students with disabilities, especially those with emotional or behavioral challenges, modeling positive emotional regulation and appropriate behavior is essential. A teacher's immersion in the classroom not only helps maintain a calm and controlled environment but also sets an example for students to emulate. Teachers who demonstrate self-regulation, patience, and empathy in their interactions with students teach critical social-emotional skills, such as conflict resolution, emotional expression, and self-awareness. These skills are essential for students in special education as they navigate social relationships, classroom routines, and everyday life. Immersion allows teachers to model these behaviors continuously, reinforcing their importance in the classroom.

Fostering Strong Teacher-Student Relationships (O'Connor & McCartney, 2007; Darling-Hammond et al., 2019). The teacher-student relationship is one of the most critical factors in the success of students, especially those with diverse learning needs. Being immersed in the classroom helps build strong, meaningful connections between educators and students. When teachers invest in their students emotionally and intellectually, students are more likely to feel valued and respected, which in turn fosters a sense of belonging and academic confidence. A strong relationship with a teacher can be especially transformative for students with disabilities, as they may have experienced a history of frustration or failure in the educational system. Immersed teachers demonstrate care and commitment to their students' growth, both academically and personally, helping them build resilience and self-esteem.

Improving Classroom Management (Dawes et al., 2024; Kline, 2023). Classroom management is often a challenge especially when students may have diverse needs, including behavioral or attention challenges. A teacher who is immersed in the classroom is better equipped to manage behavior effectively by recognizing early signs of disruption and addressing them before they escalate. Immersion enables teachers to notice subtle cues that may indicate a student's distress or disengagement, allowing for timely interventions that prevent behavioral issues from interfering with learning. Teachers who are present in the moment can establish clear expectations, provide consistent feedback, and reinforce positive behaviors, thereby promoting a well-structured and supportive classroom environment.

Promoting Student Independence and Self-Advocacy (Ma, 2021; Hu et al., 2023). When educators are deeply immersed in teaching, they create an environment that encourages students to develop independence and self-advocacy. Immersed teachers are more likely to notice opportunities to empower students to take control of their learning, ask for help when needed, and make choices in their educational journey. In special education, where students often need explicit instruction in self-advocacy and independence, the teacher's immersion provides the consistent support necessary to nurture these skills. Through individualized attention, teachers can guide students in setting personal goals, problem-solving challenges, and learning to communicate their needs effectively. These skills are invaluable in helping students navigate both their academic and personal lives.

Implementing Teacher Immersion

Active Listening and Observation. One of the core aspects of being fully immersed in teaching is active listening and keen observation. Teachers must focus on understanding each student's unique needs, preferences, and learning styles. Active listening involves not only hearing what students say but also observing their nonverbal cues and emotional states. Teachers can use this information to adjust lessons and provide targeted support, ensuring that each student feels heard and understood. Regular observations also allow teachers to track progress, identify potential challenges, and celebrate successes, reinforcing a positive learning environment.

Adapting Instruction in Real Time. Immersion allows teachers to make adjustments to instruction in real time based on students' responses and needs. Special education classrooms often require dynamic and flexible teaching strategies, as students may learn at different rates or respond better to alternative teaching methods. Being immersed in the classroom means being responsive to the moment—changing lesson plans, offering additional support, or providing alternative learning materials to meet the diverse needs of students. This flexibility helps ensure that all students are engaged, challenged, and supported appropriately.

Building a Classroom Culture of Empathy and Understanding. An immersive teaching approach fosters a classroom culture of empathy and mutual respect. Teachers can cultivate this environment by actively engaging with students, learning about their individual experiences, and recognizing their unique strengths and challenges. Through immersion, teachers can help build a community where students feel safe to share their thoughts, feelings, and struggles. This sense of community can lead to greater cooperation, peer support, and a more inclusive learning environment, where all students feel valued and supported.

Consistent Reflection and Self-Assessment. To maintain immersion, teachers must regularly reflect on their own practices and effectiveness. This involves assessing whether they are truly present with their students, recognizing individual needs, and responding with intention. Ongoing reflection allows for meaningful adjustments in teaching approach, ensuring that instruction remains responsive and relevant to a diverse range of learners. One powerful—and courageous—way to deepen this process is by inviting direct feedback. If you're brave enough, consider creating a brief survey for your students to evaluate your teaching methods. It requires vulnerability, but the insights can be both eye-opening and transformative. Ultimately, this commitment to self-assessment supports professional growth and helps teachers sustain an engaged, focused, and impactful classroom presence.

Student Feedback Survey
Your honest feedback helps me improve our class experience. Thank you for sharing!

1. What helps you learn best in this class?
   (Open-ended)
2. Is there anything I could do differently to help you understand the material better?
   (Open-ended)
3. How comfortable do you feel asking for help when you're confused?

   - Very comfortable
   - Somewhat comfortable
   - Not very comfortable
   - Not comfortable at all

4. Do the activities in class feel engaging and interesting to you?

   - Always
   - Often
   - Sometimes
   - Rarely
   - Never

5. What's one thing I do as a teacher that really helps you learn?
   (Open-ended)

Bringing Learning to Life

The majority of my teaching career has been spent with students who others often describe as "challenging"—many with emotional impairments, or on the autism spectrum, often nonverbal, and frequently exhibiting behaviors that made learning difficult to access in traditional ways. Attention spans were short, communication was unpredictable, and yet, these were the students who taught me the most about connection.

As human beings, we all crave connection. When we feel safe in a relationship, real connection follows. It's that sense of emotional safety that makes a relationship feel rooted and secure—and our students need that just as much as we do.

One of the most powerful ways we can give it to them is by being fully immersed in their learning experience. Not just present—*immersed*. This isn't something that takes weeks or months to build. It's a daily decision, an intentional mindset: to show up, to tune in, and to meet our students exactly where they are. And yes—it's exhausting. But the impact it can have is immeasurable. I've seen it, especially in my work with students on the spectrum.

Not long ago, I was working alongside the autism specialist in a Midwestern school district, visiting several self-contained classrooms as part of the *Hocus Focus* project—a magic-trick-themed supplemental curriculum designed specifically for special education. One morning, I knocked on the door of a classroom, and the teacher stepped into the hallway to "prepare" me. She explained, somewhat cautiously, that this was a self-contained classroom—emphasizing that all of the students were on the autism spectrum, most nonverbal, and all with significant needs. And then she asked me the question that still stays with me: *"Do you still want to come in?"*

It was clear that there'd been a disconnect—no one had told her that I was *there* for her students. With a big smile, I assured her, "Absolutely—I can't wait to meet them."

As I stepped into the room, I saw the students seated at a table with their aides nearby. I took my time. I crouched down, introduced myself one by one, speaking quietly, arms extended, palms up. Each student placed their small hands in mine, looked into my eyes, and welcomed me into their space. That moment of mutual respect—of invitation—was everything.

I stood and said good morning. A small voice from across the room echoed back, "Good morning." Then I pulled out a small bouquet of feather flowers. Immediately, one student called out "yellow"—the exact color of the flowers. The teacher's head whipped around, eyes wide in disbelief.

I showed them how to make "pinchers" with their thumb and index finger and demonstrated how to pluck a flower and drop it in the bag. One by one, they mirrored my motion—some miming the action in the air, others gently reaching for the flowers. One little girl whispered "yellow," smelled the flower deeply, then dropped it in the bag. It was beautiful.

Then came the magic. I invited them to wave their hands while I said the magic word, "abracadabra." As they did, the bush bloomed again—this time with different colored flowers. "Orange!" one called out. "Purple!" said another. We went around again, naming colors, choosing favorites, smelling each bloom before dropping it in the bag. Smiles were growing wider, voices more confident.

We did it one more time. And this time, several students joined in with "abracadabra" as the bush blossomed with bright red flowers. Laughter and applause erupted. "Red flowers!" they shouted, beaming.

The teacher told me afterward that this was the most engaged she had ever seen them. If you work with these students, you already know this: connection doesn't come from curriculum. It comes from presence. It comes from showing up again and again, completely immersed in the moment. For students like these—especially when time is limited—I have to be *all in* during every second we have together. And when I am, the results are nothing short of magic.

Summary

Being fully immersed in the special education classroom is essential for fostering meaningful learning experiences for students with disabilities. Immersion builds trust, increases engagement, and creates an environment where students feel safe, respected, and supported. By actively listening, adapting instruction, and modeling positive behaviors, teachers can establish strong relationships with their students, promote independence, and enhance academic success. Implementing immersion in the classroom requires teachers to be fully present, observant, and flexible, continuously adapting their approaches to meet the diverse needs of their students. This approach not only enhances learning outcomes but also contributes to the overall well-being of students, helping them navigate the challenges of both the classroom and the world beyond.

 **Discussion Questions**

1. How does your ability to be immersed in your classroom impact students with diverse learning needs, and what specific strategies can you use to enhance their immersion?
2. In what ways can being fully immersed in the classroom help build trust and emotional safety for your students, particularly those who have experienced trauma or adversity?
3. What are the potential risks or challenges you may face when striving to be fully present with their students, and how can you overcome these challenges to maintain engagement?
4. How can your immersion in the learning process improve classroom management and student behavior, especially in special education settings where students may have unique emotional or behavioral challenges?
5. What role does teacher immersion play in fostering student independence and self-advocacy, and how can you balance providing support while encouraging these skills in your students?

References

Allen, K. A., Kern, M. L., Vella-Brodrick, D., Hattie, J., & Waters, L. (2018). School belonging: A review of the history, current trends, and future directions. *Educational and Developmental Psychologist, 35*(1), 1–12. https://doi.org/10.1017/edp.2018.6

Burke Harris, N. (2018). *The deepest well: Healing the long-term effects of childhood adversity*. Houghton Mifflin Harcourt.

Craig, S. E. (2016). *Creating trauma-sensitive schools: A guide for school social workers and educators*. Oxford University Press.

Darling-Hammond, L., Flook, L., Cook-Harvey, C., Barron, B., & Osher, D. (2019). Implications for educational practice of the science of learning and development. *Applied Developmental Science, 24*(2), 97–140. https://doi.org/10.1080/10888691.2018.1537791

Dawes, M., Sterrett, B. I., Brooks, D. S., Lee, D. L., Hamm, J. V., & Farmer, T. W. (2024). Enhancing teachers' capacity to manage classroom behavior as a means to reduce burnout: Directed consultation, supported professionalism, and the BASE model. *Journal of Emotional and Behavioral Disorders, 32*(2), 110–123. https://doi.org/10.1177/10634266241235154

Hu, Z., Shan, N., & Jiao, R. (2023). The relationships between perceived teacher autonomy support, academic self-efficacy, and learning engagement among primary school students: A network analysis. *European Journal of Psychology of Education, 39*(2), 503–516. https://doi.org/10.1007/s10212-023-00703-7

Jennings, P. A., & Greenberg, M. T. (2009). The prosocial classroom: Teacher social and emotional competence in relation to student and classroom outcomes. *Review of Educational Research, 79*(1), 491–525. https://doi.org/10.3102/0034654308325693

Kline, R. B. (2023). Teaching presence promotes learner affective engagement: The roles of cognitive load and need for cognition. *Computers in Human Behavior, 143*, 107703. Article 107703. https://doi.org/10.1016/j.chb.2023.107703

Ma, Q. (2021). The role of teacher autonomy support on students' academic engagement and resilience. *Frontiers in Psychology, 12*, Article 778581. https://doi.org/10.3389/fpsyg.2021.778581

Mitchell, R. M., Kensler, L. A. W., & Tschannen-Moran, M. (2018). Student trust in teachers and student perceptions of safety: Positive predictors of student identification with school. *International Journal of Leadership in Education, 21*(2), 135–154. https://doi.org/10.1080/13603124.2016.1157211

O'Connor, E. E., & McCartney, K. (2007). The contribution of middle childhood teacher-student relationships to educational outcomes in early adolescence. *Journal of School Psychology, 45*(3), 211–229. https://doi.org/10.1016/j.jsp.2006.05.005

Overstreet, S., & Chafouleas, S. M. (2016). Trauma-informed schools: Introduction to the special issue. *School Mental Health, 8*(1), 1–6. https://doi.org/10.1007/s12310-016-9184-1

Pedler, M., Hudson, S., & Yeigh, T. (2020). The teachers' role in student engagement: A review. *Australian Journal of Teacher Education, 45*(3), 48–62. https://doi.org/10.14221/ajte.2020v45n3.3

Pianta, R. C. (1999). *Enhancing relationships between children and teachers*. American Psychological Association. https://doi.org/10.1037/10314-000

Schonert-Reichl, K. A. (2017). Social and emotional learning and teachers. *The Future of Children, 27*(1), 137–155. https://doi.org/10.1353/foc.2017.0007

Tomlinson, C. A. (2014). *The differentiated classroom: Responding to the needs of all learners* (2nd ed.). Association for Supervision and Curriculum Development (ASCD).

Wentzel, K. R. (2010). Students' relationships with teachers as motivational contexts. In T. Urdan & S. Karabenick (Eds.), *Advances in motivation and achievement* (Vol. 11, pp. 135–167). Emerald Group.

7

A is for Affirmation

> You are special. You're my friend. You are a very special person.
>
> Fred Rogers (Mr. Rogers)

The power of affirmation cannot be underestimated in the success of our students. Children and adolescents (and adults) have an innate need for attachment, acceptance, and affirmation. We are biologically wired to connect to one another using sound. Our soft, subtle, sincere words of affirmation can be extremely motivating, encouraging, and stabilizing. These words tell our students they are seen, heard, and valued. Offering positive affirmation is an essential practice that can significantly impact student growth and development. Encouraging words often make the difference between success and failure. As Maya Angelou so beautifully reminds us, "I've learned that people will forget what you said, people will forget what you did, but people will never forget how you made them feel."

Consistent encouragement and recognition of our students' efforts can boost self-esteem, motivation, and a sense of belonging. Positive affirmation helps create an environment where they feel valued and supported, regardless of the challenges they may face. By affirming students' strengths, achievements, and progress—no matter how small—teachers can foster resilience, build confidence, and inspire a growth mindset. In special education, where students often encounter obstacles that may hinder their academic and emotional progress, positive affirmation serves as a powerful tool to reinforce their potential, helping them navigate their learning journey with optimism and determination.

The Value and Implementation of Offering Positive Affirmation

Many of our students often face unique challenges that can affect their self-esteem, motivation, and overall sense of worth. The importance of positive affirmation in this context cannot be overstated. Positive affirmation—acknowledging students' strengths, progress, and efforts—plays a crucial role in fostering a supportive and encouraging learning environment. By offering consistent, genuine affirmation, educators can help students build confidence, develop resilience, and stay motivated to overcome obstacles. In this chapter, we will explore the value of offering positive affirmation in our classrooms, followed by practical strategies for implementing it effectively.

The Value of Positive Affirmation

Boosting Self-Esteem and Confidence (Kadian, 2023; Manning, 2019). Students often face challenges that can make them feel different or less capable than their peers. For many, this can lead to low self-esteem and a lack of confidence in their abilities. Offering positive affirmation helps counteract these negative feelings by reinforcing the idea that their efforts are valued. When teachers acknowledge progress—whether it's mastering a new skill, making an improvement, or simply putting in consistent effort—students begin to see themselves as capable learners. This affirmation boosts their confidence and helps them develop a stronger sense of self-worth.

Promoting a Growth Mindset (Kadian, 2023; Manning, 2019). When learning challenges are more pronounced, it's easy for students to feel discouraged or defeated when they struggle. However, positive affirmation can help shift their perspective.

By praising effort, perseverance, and progress rather than just results, teachers encourage students to view challenges as opportunities for growth rather than insurmountable obstacles. This approach fosters a growth mindset, where students understand that abilities can improve over time through effort and practice. Students who embrace a growth mindset are more likely to persevere through difficulties, take risks, and be motivated to continue learning, knowing that their effort will lead to improvement.

Strengthening Emotional Resilience (Escobar-Soler et al., 2023). Positive affirmation not only builds students' academic skills but also strengthens their emotional resilience. Our students with diverse learning needs often encounter setbacks that can be discouraging, whether it's a learning difficulty, social challenges, or behavioral struggles. Consistent affirmation helps students develop the emotional tools to cope with frustration and setbacks. When students are praised for their resilience, perseverance, and effort, they are more likely to internalize these qualities and apply them in future challenges. This process helps them understand that setbacks are a natural part of the learning process, and with persistence, they can overcome them.

Creating a Supportive and Inclusive Classroom Environment (Manning, 2019; Yeager & Dweck, 2012). Inclusion is a core principle of education, and offering positive affirmation is key to creating an environment that truly embraces all students, regardless of their individual challenges. When educators consistently affirm students, they contribute to a classroom culture where every student feels valued and accepted. This inclusive atmosphere fosters positive relationships among peers and helps students with disabilities feel like active participants in the classroom community. When students feel supported and recognized for their unique strengths, they are more likely to engage with their peers and participate in classroom activities.

Increasing Motivation and Engagement (Cents-Boonstra et al., 2020; Zhang, 2014) Positive affirmation plays a crucial role in maintaining student motivation and engagement, especially for our diverse learners. When students are consistently acknowledged for their efforts, they are more likely to feel motivated to continue working hard. This sense of recognition reinforces the idea that their contributions matter, which encourages further participation and effort. For students who may struggle to stay engaged, affirmation can be a powerful tool to help them remain focused and committed to their learning goals. Additionally, praise and affirmation can serve as a form of positive reinforcement, motivating students to continue exhibiting positive behaviors and academic progress.

Implementing Positive Affirmation

Be Specific and Genuine in Your Praise. To be effective, positive affirmation must be specific and sincere. General or vague praise such as "Good job" can feel hollow to students and may not convey the importance of their individual efforts. Instead, teachers should focus on specific actions, improvements, or behaviors. For example, rather than simply saying, "You did great," a teacher might say, "I'm really impressed with how you kept going, even when the task became difficult. Your perseverance is truly inspiring." This specific praise acknowledges the effort and determination behind the student's actions, which is more meaningful and motivating.

Praise Effort, Not Just Achievement. Many of our students face difficulties in mastering academic content, and success may look different for each individual. Therefore, it is essential to praise effort and progress, not just final outcomes. Focusing on effort emphasizes that learning is a process, and improvement is always possible. For example, instead of only congratulating a student for correctly solving a math problem, a teacher might say, "I noticed how hard you worked through each step of the problem. That's the kind of persistence that leads to success." This type of affirmation encourages students to see their effort as valuable, regardless of the result.

Affirm Small Successes. Celebrating small successes can have a profound impact on students' motivation and self-esteem. Teachers should be proactive in recognizing these milestones, no matter how small they may seem. In special education, progress may be incremental, but each step forward is significant.

Whether a student improves their handwriting, answers a question correctly, or follows instructions more effectively, these small achievements are worthy of affirmation. By acknowledging these successes, teachers reinforce the idea that progress is being made and that the student's efforts are recognized.

Incorporate Affirmation into Daily Routines. Offering positive affirmation should be a regular and consistent practice, integrated into the daily routines of the classroom. Teachers can use affirmation during transitions, group work, one-on-one interactions, and in response to both academic and behavioral efforts. Consistency is key in building a positive classroom environment where students feel continually supported. Positive affirmations can be delivered verbally, through written notes, or even with nonverbal gestures such as a thumbs-up or high-five. The regularity of these affirmations helps reinforce a supportive classroom culture.

Ensure Affirmation Is Tailored to Individual Needs. Different students may respond to different types of affirmation. Some students may prefer verbal praise, while others may appreciate written feedback or recognition in front of the class. It's important for teachers to get to know their students and tailor affirmation to their preferences. Additionally, some students may need more frequent or more targeted affirmation to feel supported. For instance, a student who struggles with emotional regulation may benefit from affirmation that focuses on their ability to manage frustration, while a student with a learning disability may benefit from affirmation centered on their persistence in completing tasks.

Encourage Peer Affirmation. In addition to teacher-directed affirmation, peer-to-peer affirmation can also be powerful in fostering a positive classroom environment. Encouraging students to recognize and affirm each other's efforts helps build a supportive, inclusive community. Teachers can create opportunities for students to share compliments, celebrate each other's successes, or offer encouragement when peers face challenges. This peer affirmation can enhance students' social-emotional skills, such as empathy and cooperation, while also reinforcing the classroom's sense of community and belonging.

Bringing Learning to Life

During my adventures teaching middle school students, I had one whose presence filled the room—not with enthusiasm for learning but with a defiant, dismissive attitude that she wore like armor. She was sharp, quick-witted, and made it clear from day 1 that she had no interest in being part of the classroom experience. She wasn't loud or disruptive in a traditional sense—she was coolly disengaged, and her attitude had a way of influencing those around her. But I've always believed that behavior is a form of communication. So instead of reacting with frustration, I found myself asking: *"What is she trying to tell me?"*

Over the first few days of class, I became an observer. I paid close attention to her interactions with peers, how she moved through the room, and the subtle shifts in her posture when she was interested versus when she was checked out. I noticed that, every now and then, something would catch her attention—an activity, a topic, a challenge—and her guard would drop just slightly.

So I started with something small. When I saw a moment of effort or curiosity, I'd walk by her desk, give it a light tap, and say quietly, "I appreciate how engaged you are right now." The first time, she looked up at me with a mix of confusion and suspicion. But I kept doing it. By the fourth or fifth time, I caught a flicker of a smile.

Over time, those moments grew. I continued to offer encouragement—genuine, specific, and consistent. As her confidence grew, so did her engagement. By the middle of the semester, she was a different student. She volunteered answers, supported classmates, and began offering her own quiet affirmations to others. She had found her voice—not as a resistor but as a leader.

That experience reminded me how powerful subtle, intentional affirmation can be—especially when we use it to support effort, not just outcomes. Every student carries a story into our classrooms. Sometimes, all it takes is a moment of being seen for that story to begin to change…and that's the power of positive affirmation.

Summary

Offering positive affirmation is an essential and powerful tool in the classroom. By affirming students' efforts, progress, and individual strengths, educators help build their self-esteem, motivation, and resilience. Positive affirmation fosters a growth mindset, creates an inclusive classroom environment, and increases student engagement. Implementing positive affirmation requires specificity, consistency, and a deep understanding of each student's unique needs and preferences. Through thoughtful and tailored praise, teachers can empower students to face challenges with confidence and determination, ultimately supporting their academic and emotional growth.

 **Discussion Questions**

1. Why is it especially important for you to use positive affirmation with students, and how can it influence their self-esteem and motivation?
2. How does praising effort over achievement contribute to developing a growth mindset in your diverse learners? Can you share examples where this approach made a difference in your classroom or experience?
3. What strategies can you use to make sure youyour affirmations are specific, sincere, and tailored to individual students" needs and preferences?
4. How can you celebrate small successes in meaningful ways that will support long-term academic and emotional growth? Why is recognizing these moments essential in special education?
5. What are some effective methods you can use to encourage peer affirmation, and how can this practice contribute to building a more inclusive and supportive classroom community?

References

Cents-Boonstra, M., Lichtwarck-Aschoff, A., Denessen, E., Aelterman, N., & Haerens, L. (2020). Fostering student engagement with motivating teaching: An observation study of teacher and student behaviors. *Learning and Instruction, 67*, 101313.

Escobar-Soler, C., Berrios, R., Peñaloza-Díaz, G., Melis-Rivera, C., Caqueo-Urízar, A., Ponce-Correa, F., & Flores, J. (2023). Effectiveness of self-affirmation interventions in educational settings: A meta-analysis. *Healthcare, 12*(1), 3. https://doi.org/10.3390/healthcare12010003

Kadian, A. (2023). The use of positive affirmations in increasing self-esteem. *International Journal for Multidisciplinary Research, 5*(4), 2254–2258. https://www.ijfmr.com/papers/2023/4/4348.pdf

Manning, R. (2019). The impact of positive affirmations on the self-confidence levels of adolescent girls. *Psychologia: Journal of Psychological Research, 14*(2), 89–97. https://psychologia.pelnus.ac.id/index.php/Psychologia/article/view/69

Yeager, D. S., & Dweck, C. S. (2012). Mindsets that promote resilience: When students believe that personal characteristics are mutable. *Educational Psychologist, 47*(4), 302–314. https://doi.org/10.1080/00461520.2012.722805

Zhang, J. (2014). The role of teachers in motivating students to learn. *Journal of College Teaching & Learning, 11*(2), 123–130.

8

N is for Natural Rapport

No significant learning happens without a significant relationship.
— Dr. James Comer, American psychiatrist and educator

Every child deserves a champion—an adult who will never give up on them, who understands the power of connection, and insists they become the best that they can possibly be.
— Rita Pierson, Educator

Being immersed with students and building a natural rapport with them are two distinct but complementary aspects of teaching. *Immersion* refers to being fully present and engaged in the moment with your students during lessons or activities. It involves focusing all your attention on the students' needs, actions, and responses, creating an atmosphere of trust and security. An immersed teacher adapts to the dynamic classroom environment, reacting immediately to student behaviors, emotions, and learning cues. This creates a stable, responsive, and supportive environment, which is crucial in maintaining engagement and fostering positive learning experiences.

On the other hand, *building rapport* is about developing a genuine, trusting relationship over time. It's the foundation of positive interactions, where the teacher takes time to understand students' individual needs, interests, and personalities. A teacher who builds rapport connects with students on a personal level, making them feel valued and respected. This connection lays the groundwork for effective communication, cooperation, and emotional safety within the classroom.

While immersion is about being actively present in the moment, rapport-building is a longer-term process that involves consistent effort in understanding and connecting with students on an emotional and personal level. Both are vital for creating an optimal learning environment, especially in special education, where emotional support and trust are as important as academic instruction.

At the heart of Natural Rapport is getting to know your students on a personal level, showing them they are more than just a grade, and giving them a safe, fun environment sets that the stage for learning. Developing a genuine, trusting relationship with each student helps create a safe and supportive learning environment. A teacher who connects with students on a personal level can foster open communication, motivate students to engage, and provide individualized support that promotes both academic and social development. In this context, rapport-building is not just about creating a positive atmosphere—it's about empowering students to thrive despite their challenges.

The Value and Implementation of Building Natural Rapport

The relationships between teachers and students are fundamental to creating a positive, productive, and supportive learning environment. Building natural rapport is a crucial part of these relationships. Rapport refers to the bond of mutual respect, trust, and understanding that forms between individuals. When teachers take the time to build rapport with their students, they are creating the foundation for effective teaching and learning. A teacher's ability to connect with students in a meaningful way helps to reduce anxiety, increase engagement, and improve overall learning outcomes.

The Value of Building Natural Rapport

Fostering Trust and Safety (Brunzell et al., 2015; Zhou, 2021). Trust is at the core of any positive relationship, and it is especially important for students with disabilities, who may have experienced past failures or frustration in the educational system. When students feel that their teacher understands and respects them, they are more likely to feel safe, both emotionally and academically. A trusting relationship creates a classroom atmosphere where students are willing to take risks, ask questions, and express their challenges without fear of judgment. This safety is crucial for our students, especially those who may face additional social and emotional barriers to learning.

Enhancing Communication (Moody, 2019; Zhou, 2021). Building rapport helps improve communication between teachers and students. Clear and open communication is essential for addressing individual needs and concerns. When a teacher develops a strong rapport with a student, the student feels more comfortable sharing their struggles, needs, or ideas. In turn, teachers can better adapt their teaching strategies and support the student in ways that are most effective for them. This kind of communication also extends beyond verbal exchanges—teachers who are attuned to the emotional and behavioral cues of their students can identify when a student is frustrated, overwhelmed, or disengaged, allowing for timely and appropriate interventions.

Increasing Motivation and Engagement (American Psychological Association, 2025; Bardorfer & Dolenc, 2022; Strachan, 2021; Zhou, 2021). When students feel that their teacher genuinely cares about them and their success, they are more motivated to participate in class activities. In special education, where students may struggle with focus, attention, or confidence, this motivation is especially important. Building rapport encourages students to feel that their effort is recognized and valued, which can increase their willingness to engage in learning tasks. For example, a student who feels a personal connection to the teacher is more likely to put forth effort during challenging assignments, knowing they are supported and encouraged.

Promoting Emotional and Social Development (Kim, 2020; Rimm-Kaufman, 2025; Poulou, 2017). Building rapport is not just about academic success; it also plays a critical role in fostering emotional and social growth. Many of our diverse learners may have difficulties with social skills, emotional regulation, or forming relationships with peers. A teacher who takes the time to understand each student's personality, preferences, and needs can guide them in developing these essential skills. By providing consistent support and feedback in a nurturing and non-judgmental environment, teachers can help students build emotional resilience, empathy, and social competence.

Individualizing Instruction and Support (Bardorfer & Dolenc, 2022; Zhou, 2021). Each student in a classroom has unique needs, strengths, and challenges. Building rapport allows teachers to better understand these individual characteristics and tailor their instruction accordingly. Whether it's adjusting teaching methods, providing accommodations, or offering emotional support, the rapport built with students enables teachers to identify the most effective strategies to support their growth. This individualized attention is critical for ensuring that all students, regardless of their challenges, have the opportunity to succeed.

Implementation of Building Natural Rapport

Active Listening. One of the most important ways to build rapport with students is through active listening. Teachers can show students that they value their thoughts and feelings by giving them their full attention and responding appropriately. Active listening involves not only hearing what the student says but also understanding the underlying emotions and needs. This kind of engagement lets students know that their voices are heard and that their concerns are taken seriously. Active listening also promotes a deeper understanding of each student's perspective, allowing the teacher to tailor their support more effectively.

Consistent and Positive Communication. Positive communication is essential for building rapport. Teachers should strive to use language that is encouraging, respectful, and empathetic. This includes providing positive reinforcement, acknowledging students' efforts, and celebrating their successes. In addition to verbal communication, teachers can use body language and nonverbal cues to show engagement and attentiveness. Smiling, maintaining eye contact, and using open and welcoming gestures can all contribute to building rapport and creating a safe, welcoming classroom environment.

Personalizing Interactions. Each student in a classroom is an individual with their own preferences, interests, and learning styles. Building rapport involves getting to know these personal aspects of each student's life. Teachers can learn about their students' interests by asking questions, observing their behavior, or using tools like student surveys. For example, a teacher might find out that a student loves animals or enjoys a particular hobby and can use that information to create learning experiences that connect with the student's interests. By acknowledging these personal details, teachers make students feel seen and valued, reinforcing the sense of connection between them.

Creating a Safe and Supportive Environment. A crucial aspect of rapport-building is ensuring that the classroom environment is emotionally safe for all students. Teachers can create a positive space by promoting inclusivity, encouraging collaboration, and addressing conflicts with sensitivity and fairness. It is essential that students feel free to express themselves without fear of criticism or ridicule. This environment can be fostered through clear and consistent classroom rules, routines, and expectations, which help students feel secure and understand what is expected of them.

Demonstrating Empathy and Patience. Students often face difficulties that go beyond academic challenges, such as social and emotional struggles or behavioral issues. To build rapport, teachers must approach these challenges with empathy and patience. Understanding that students may have different emotional or developmental needs, and showing genuine concern for their well-being, helps establish a strong teacher-student bond. Teachers should also be patient, allowing students to express themselves and work through difficulties at their own pace. Demonstrating that the teacher is there to support them, regardless of their struggles, fosters trust and strengthens the rapport.

Being Consistent and Reliable. Consistency is key in building rapport. Students often thrive in structured environments where they know what to expect. Teachers who are consistent in their interactions, responses, and expectations help students feel more secure and valued. Consistent communication, follow-through on promises, and reliable emotional support all contribute to building a strong relationship based on trust and reliability. When students know that their teacher will be there for them, they are more likely to feel comfortable and open in the classroom.

Bringing Learning to Life

If there's one key idea I hope resonates from this chapter, it's the importance of moving beyond surface-level presence in the classroom and into the space of authentic, meaningful rapport with your students. True rapport isn't just about showing up—it's about showing *interest*. It's built over time through small, consistent actions: asking how a student's day is going, remembering what artist they're listening to, or what show they're currently into. These seemingly minor moments of connection communicate something powerful: *I see you, and I care about who you are.*

I've been fortunate to teach so many incredible students over the years, and it's that intentional rapport-building that has had the greatest impact on both our relationships and their learning outcomes. One student who really stands out to me is Ethan.

Ethan had been diagnosed with high-functioning autism (formerly Asperger's), ADHD, and sensory processing disorder. He had a sharp mind, a wonderfully quirky sense of humor, and a tendency to laugh at his own jokes—something I came to appreciate more and more. He was thoughtful and insightful, but he needed extra time to process information. That wasn't always well understood by those around him.

Ethan often felt rushed—by his peers and sometimes by well-meaning teachers who were just trying to keep things moving.

But that pressure only left him frustrated, and in some cases, completely shut down. What I learned, though, was that when you gave him the time he needed—*really* gave it to him—his responses were not only accurate, but often imaginative and creative. He would light up when he figured something out, sometimes bursting into laughter and rushing over to share his discovery with me.

What began as simple patience on my part gradually transformed into something much more meaningful. By giving Ethan the time and space he needed to process information, I was also giving myself the opportunity to truly *know* him—not just as a student, but as a person.

During lunch or recess, we'd sometimes walk the perimeter of the playground together. I'd gently encourage him to join the other kids, but more often than not, he'd eventually circle back to my desk, sometimes with a small token in hand—something he'd picked up or made, a quiet gesture of connection.

One day, he confided in me: "You're the only one who really takes the time to understand me." He told me how much he appreciated that I waited for his answers, that I asked questions not just about school, but about the things that mattered to him—his family, the music he liked, the Netflix shows he was watching, even how many friends he had on Instagram. Over time, those conversations deepened. He began to share his fears and frustrations and his academic struggles and successes. He opened up about what made him angry, what made him anxious, and what he found comforting.

And then, in a moment that's stayed with me ever since, he quietly apologized for the way his ADHD sometimes made him act. That vulnerability was a turning point—not just for him, but for me. It was a reminder that when we give students time, attention, and space to be themselves, we're not just supporting their learning—we're honoring their humanity. And that, more than anything, is the foundation for meaningful education.

That's what rapport looks like—it's not always loud or obvious. Sometimes it's found in the quiet moments, in the shared understanding that learning doesn't look the same for every student and that every student has something unique and valuable to offer… if we're willing to take the time to listen.

Summary

Building natural rapport with students in special education is an essential practice for creating a positive, effective, and supportive learning environment. By fostering trust, improving communication, increasing motivation, promoting emotional growth, and individualizing support, teachers can help students thrive academically, socially, and emotionally. The implementation of rapport-building strategies—such as active listening, positive communication, personalization, and creating a safe environment—are key to cultivating meaningful and lasting connections with students. Ultimately, the rapport a teacher builds with their students serves as the foundation for all other aspects of teaching, ensuring that students feel valued, understood, and empowered to succeed.

Discussion Questions

1. How do immersion and rapport-building differ, and why are both essential in your classroom? Can you think of a moment where one supported the other?
2. In what ways can building natural rapport help foster emotional safety and trust among your students? How does this trust influence classroom behavior and participation?
3. What are some strategies you can use to personalize interactions and actively listen to students? Why is this particularly important in special education settings?
4. How can consistent and positive communication support a student's emotional and social development? Can you share an example where your words made a visible impact on a student's behavior or self-esteem?
5. Why is empathy and patience so vital in building rapport with students who face both academic and social-emotional challenges? In what ways can you balance support with maintaining expectations?

References

American Psychological Association. (2025). Improving students' relationships with teachers. https://www.apa.org/education-career/k12/relationships

Bardorfer, A., & Dolenc, K. (2022). Teacher–student rapport as predictor of learning motivation within self-determination theory. *Journal of Pedagogical Research, 6*(2), 115–133. https://www.proquest.com/openview/b324b9c6cf28d74a8850b660216a87b4/1

Brunzell, T., Waters, L., & Stokes, H. (2015). Teaching with strengths in trauma-affected students: A new approach to healing and growth in the classroom. *American Journal of Orthopsychiatry, 85*(1), 3–9. https://doi.org/10.1037/ort0000048

Kim, J. (2020). The quality of social relationships in schools and adult health: Differential effects of student–student versus student–teacher relationships. *School Psychology.* https://www.apa.org/news/press/releases/2020/10/student-teacher-relationships

Moody, J. (2019). *The impact of nonverbal immediacy and rapport-building strategies on student learning and perceptions of instructor credibility* (Master's thesis, University of Maine). University of Maine Digital Commons. https://digitalcommons.library.umaine.edu/etd/3192

Poulou, M. (2017). Teacher–student relationships, social and emotional skills, and emotional and behavioural difficulties. *International Journal of Educational Psychology, 6*(1), 1–29. https://files.eric.ed.gov/fulltext/EJ1111716.pdf

Rimm-Kaufman, S. (2025, March 5). Improving students' relationships with teachers. American Psychological Association. https://www.apa.org/education-career/k12/relationships

Strachan, L. (2021). Fostering EFL/ESL students' state motivation: The role of teacher–student rapport. *Frontiers in Psychology, 12,* 754797. https://doi.org/10.3389/fpsyg.2021.754797

Zhou, X. (2021). Toward the positive consequences of teacher–student rapport for students' academic engagement in practical instruction classrooms. *Frontiers in Psychology, 12,* Article 759785. https://doi.org/10.3389/fpsyg.2021.759785

9

Hocus Focus and Hocus Focus Analytics

> Every classroom should be a safe, fun place to learn. The Hocus Focus supplemental curriculum helps bring that concept into reality. It builds confidence and self-esteem. It allows students to see that success can be achieved through hard work and attention to task.
> —Special Education Teacher | Broken Arrow, OK

In the previous chapters, eight research-based concepts were explored for their ability to engage and inspire students while supporting stronger learning outcomes. These key ideas came together in the creation of the Hocus Focus® Supplemental Curriculum (HFSC), a program I developed to help bring those strategies into everyday classroom practice. The HFSC is a student-centered, multidisciplinary arts-themed teaching approach that incorporates magic tricks into the learning process. Each lesson is designed to provide opportunities for students to learn through modeling, coaching, and scaffolding while increasing the complexity of new tasks. Each of the eleven tricks in the semester curriculum allows students to build on previously learned knowledge. As the tricks become increasingly more difficult, it expands opportunities for creative expression and progress.

The content was developed in collaboration with experts in the fields of education, special education, and occupational therapy.

The activities are fun, exciting, and engaging for students of all ages and levels. By combining education with imagination, students have improved their abilities in planning, sequencing, organizing tasks and movements, fine motor dexterity, gross motor function, concentration/focus, memory skills, and much more.

The Power of the Arts—and Magic—in Special Education

An arts-rich educational environment supports diverse learning styles and fosters academic and personal growth for students of all abilities, including those with disabilities. Rooted in theories of multiple intelligences (Gardner, 1993) and experiential learning, the arts use sensory modalities—visual, auditory, and kinesthetic—to teach in ways that align with students' strengths (Gerber & Horoschak, 2012).

Arts integration (active learning) encourages creativity, flexible thinking, and self-expression, which lead to greater autonomy, resilience, and reduced anxiety (Eisner, 2002; Kaufman, 2017). Arts-based instruction, including storytelling, performance, and improvisation, supports cognitive development, motivation, and critical thinking. Research shows arts education improves reading, math, thinking skills, social-emotional growth, and motivation (Ruppert, 2006; Spencer, 2012).

Magic, as a multidisciplinary performing art, uniquely combines storytelling, fine motor coordination, sequencing, and theatrical presentation. When used in education, especially with students with learning differences, learning and performing magic tricks:

- ◆ Stimulates sensory engagement and creative problem-solving (Frith & Walker, 1983)
- ◆ Builds confidence, self-esteem, and teamwork (Ezell & Klein-Ezell, 2003)
- ◆ Enhances communication, motor skills, and cognition (Spencer, 2012; Spencer & Balmer, 2020)

Recent studies using the HFSC demonstrated that learning and performing magic tricks leads to measurable gains in several critical areas of student development.

Introducing Hocus Focus Analytics

To maintain relevance, arts programs must demonstrate impact on student outcomes. However, assessing progress in areas like creativity or communication remains a challenge due to a lack of appropriate tools. In 2015–2016, a study was initiated to develop a reliable tool—*Hocus Focus Analytics (HFA)*—to assess student progress across these five developmental domains: cognition, motor skills, communication, social skills, and creativity, all within a magic trick-based arts curriculum (O'Rourke et al., 2018).

Cognitive Development: Arts training improves memory, attention, executive function, and abstract thinking. Students learn better when they are curious, motivated, and actively involved in the process (Posner et al., 2008; MacLean, 2008).

Motor Development: The arts enhance both fine and gross motor skills. Magic tricks, in particular, support hand-eye coordination, sequencing, and muscle control—skills vital for occupational and physical therapy goals (Hines et al., 2018; Hines et al., 2019; Spencer, 2012; Spencer et al., 2020, Yuen et al., 2021, 2023).

Communication Development: Performance-based arts offer alternative ways for students to express themselves, especially those with communication challenges. Magic incorporates language development through storytelling and character creation (Anderson & Berry, 2017).

Social Development: Arts participation fosters peer interaction, emotional regulation, and positive identity formation. Performing magic encourages group collaboration, turn-taking, leadership, and improved social behaviors (Spencer, 2012; Duffy & Fuller, 2010; Yazici, 2017; Yuen et al., 2021, 2023).

Inspiring Growth Through Magic

A Summary of the HFA Study

The research process involved developing an initial pool of 58 items, then refining them with the help of 13 special education experts (including teachers and professors). After review, the scale was narrowed down to 35 items aligned with child development standards commonly used in special education.

Five special education teachers from diverse Midwestern schools participated, teaching 31 students aged 7–14, all with a variety of disabilities. Each week for 11 weeks, teachers used the HFSC to support student learning, focusing on skills like sequencing, problem-solving, and fine and gross motor development. Teachers assessed student performance after each trick. Data collected were analyzed to ensure the reliability of the HFA tool, ultimately demonstrating it as a strong, teacher-friendly way to track student progress in creative, hands-on learning environments.

Results: Item Analysis and Reliability of the HFA Scale

To ensure the Hocus Focus® Analytics (HFA) tool was both reliable and practical for classroom use, the research team conducted a thorough item analysis. Items were chosen based on their strong connection to the overall skill they were designed to measure. To qualify, each item needed to show a high correlation with the total score for its dimension, with no item falling below a correlation of .40.

The final item correlations were strong:

- Cognitive skills items ranged from .51 to .71
- Creative skills from .65 to .76
- Motor skills from .44 to .53
- Communication skills from .56 to .66
- Social skills from .54 to .63

In terms of overall reliability:

- The full HFA scale showed excellent internal consistency (Cronbach's alpha = .91).
- Subscale reliability was also strong:
  - Cognitive (.80)
  - Creative (.87)
  - Motor Skills (.79)
  - Social Skills (.73)
- Communication Skills had a somewhat lower reliability score (.63) but still within an acceptable range for classroom-based research.

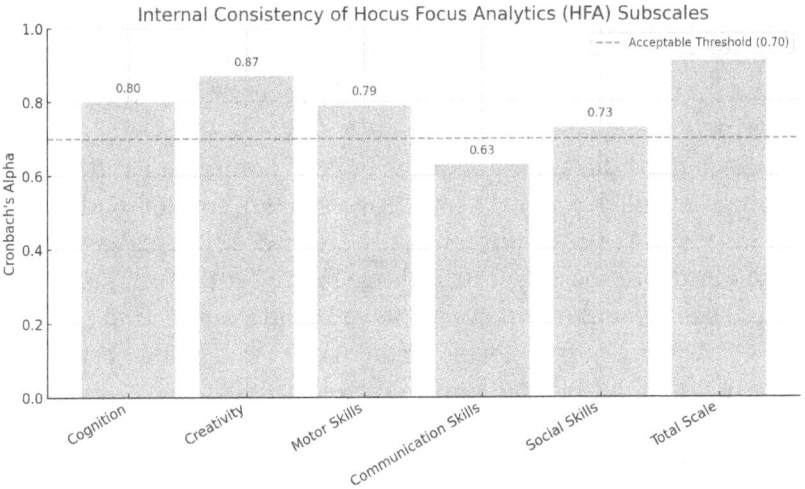

FIGURE 9.1 Chart of the internal consistency of Hocus Focus Analytics subscales.

HFA offers educators an uncomplicated, straight-forward way to track meaningful student progress in nontraditional areas often undervalued by standardized testing. It can also serve as a persuasive tool to advocate for the inclusion of arts-based programs in schools, particularly for diverse learners in inclusive classrooms.

Before beginning the assessment process, teachers input basic student information into the HFA platform, including name, gender, grade level, age, and disability classification. The system offers a user-friendly drop-down menu with multiple options, allowing educators to select one or more categories such as Autism, Speech/Language Impairment, Intellectual Disability, Learning Disability, Physical Disability, Social-Emotional Disorder, Blind/Visual Impairment, Deaf/Hearing Impairment, or None (no disability).

This comprehensive setup ensures that teachers can provide a well-rounded picture of each learner prior to evaluation. On the day of assessment, teachers simply select the student's name and date. There is also space to note any contextual factors that may influence performance—such as illness, emotional distress, or environmental disruptions—allowing for a more compassionate and accurate interpretation of progress. Teachers then indicate the type of day the student is having (excellent, good, fair, poor, or absent) before entering their ratings for each item on the HFA scale. One important feature of the platform is that all data are encrypted and only accessible to the teacher entering the data.

Once multiple assessments have been completed and saved, teachers can click on the "View Progress HFA" option within the platform. This feature automatically generates clear, easy-to-read charts and graphs that illustrate each student's progress over time. These visual reports provide valuable insights into student growth across the five developmental domains, making it easier for educators to track outcomes, share results with colleagues or families, and advocate for continued use of arts-integrated strategies in the classroom.

Potential Adaptations of the HFA Scale

The HFA tool is designed to assess task-based, performance-oriented activities, with its validation primarily focused on magic tricks. There has been some discussion about its potential application to other performance-based disciplines, such as music, dance, and drama/theater. Given that these activities are also task-based, one could argue that the tool's items may be relevant across various disciplines. Consequently, the HFA tool could potentially be adapted to track student growth and skill development in a wide range of arts-integrated experiences, offering a flexible and meaningful way to measure progress in dynamic, hands-on learning environments.

Another advantage of the HFA web-based assessment tool is its adaptability to meet the diverse needs of today's classrooms. Beyond the core HFA scale, educators have the flexibility to create and monitor their own custom goals or learning objectives. While this feature is not validated for formal use, it offers a visual representation of progress within those specific goals. This is particularly beneficial for tracking individualized student outcomes, such as IEP targets or specific classroom behaviors. Teachers can add as many personalized items as needed, and the platform will generate clear, visual charts and graphs to illustrate each student's progress over time.

HFA offers educators an uncomplicated, straight-forward way to track meaningful student progress in nontraditional areas often undervalued by standardized testing. It can also serve as a persuasive tool to advocate for the inclusion of arts-based programs in schools, particularly for diverse learners in inclusive classrooms.

Before beginning the assessment process, teachers input basic student information into the HFA platform, including name, gender, grade level, age, and disability classification. The system offers a user-friendly drop-down menu with multiple options, allowing educators to select one or more categories such as Autism, Speech/Language Impairment, Intellectual Disability, Learning Disability, Physical Disability, Social-Emotional Disorder, Blind/Visual Impairment, Deaf/Hearing Impairment, or None (no disability).

This comprehensive setup ensures that teachers can provide a well-rounded picture of each learner prior to evaluation. On the day of assessment, teachers simply select the student's name and date. There is also space to note any contextual factors that may influence performance—such as illness, emotional distress, or environmental disruptions—allowing for a more compassionate and accurate interpretation of progress. Teachers then indicate the type of day the student is having (excellent, good, fair, poor, or absent) before entering their ratings for each item on the HFA scale. One important feature of the platform is that all data are encrypted and only accessible to the teacher entering the data.

Once multiple assessments have been completed and saved, teachers can click on the "View Progress HFA" option within the platform. This feature automatically generates clear, easy-to-read charts and graphs that illustrate each student's progress over time. These visual reports provide valuable insights into student growth across the five developmental domains, making it easier for educators to track outcomes, share results with colleagues or families, and advocate for continued use of arts-integrated strategies in the classroom.

Potential Adaptations of the Hocus Focus Analytics Scale

The HFA tool is designed to assess task-based, performance-oriented activities, with its validation primarily focused on magic tricks. There has been some discussion about its potential application to other performance-based disciplines, such as music, dance, and drama/theater. Given that these activities are also task-based, one could argue that the tool's items may be relevant across various disciplines. Consequently, the HFA tool could potentially be adapted to track student growth and skill development in a wide range of arts-integrated experiences, offering a flexible and meaningful way to measure progress in dynamic, hands-on learning environments.

Another advantage of the HFA web-based assessment tool is its adaptability to meet the diverse needs of today's classrooms. Beyond the core HFA scale, educators have the flexibility to create and monitor their own custom goals or learning objectives. While this feature is not validated for formal use, it offers a visual representation of progress within those specific goals. This is particularly beneficial for tracking individualized student outcomes, such as IEP targets or specific classroom behaviors. Teachers can add as many personalized items as needed, and the platform will generate clear, visual charts and graphs to illustrate each student's progress over time.

In an educational landscape heavily influenced by standardized assessments that determine funding and programming, it is crucial to recognize the arts as an effective instructional method that enhances student learning outcomes beyond the arts themselves. The HFA scale equips educators with a compelling tool to advocate for the benefits of multidisciplinary, arts-integrated curricula, helping to persuade decision-makers responsible for budget and resource allocation to invest in diverse and inclusive educational strategies.

Bringing Learning to Life

Every classroom should be a safe, fun place to learn. The HFSC helps bring that concept into reality. It builds confidence and

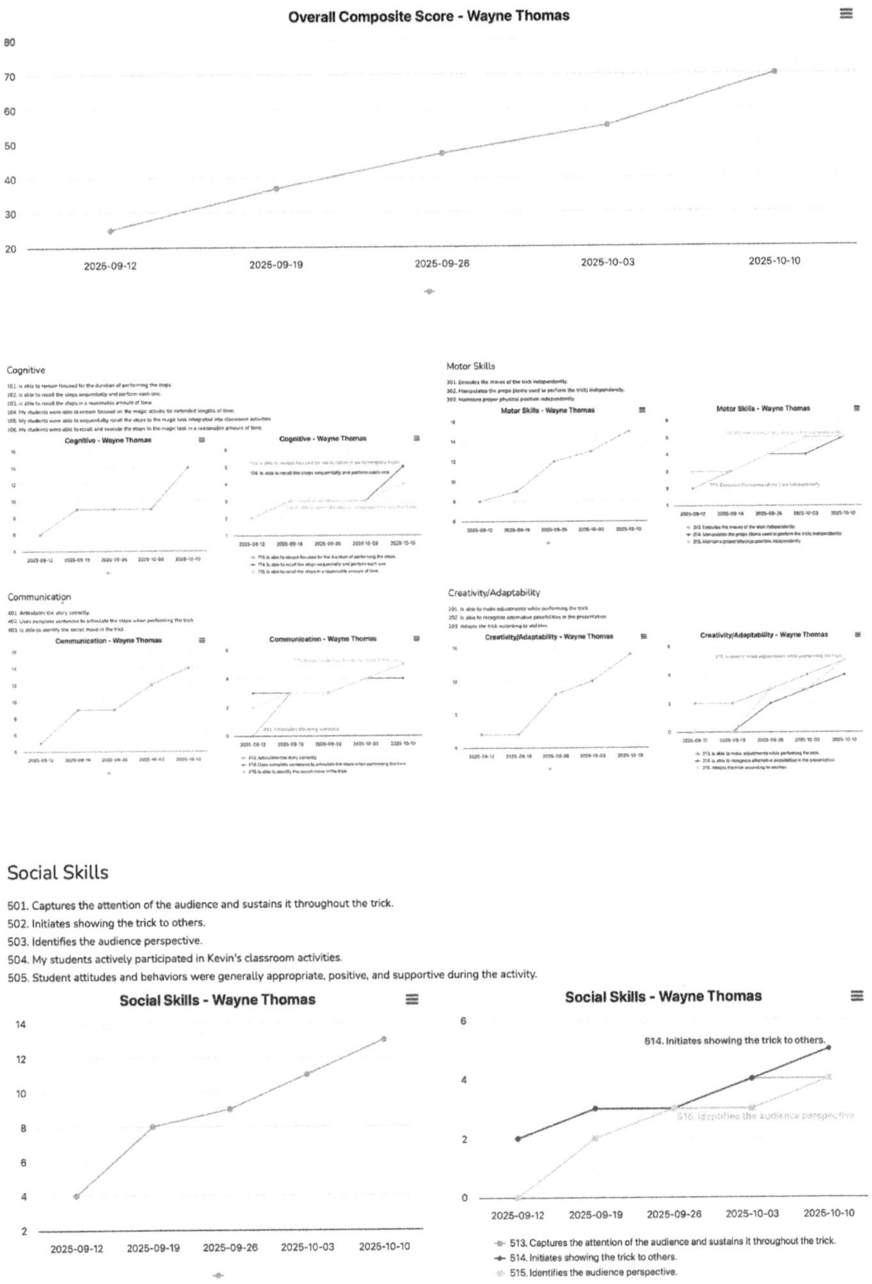

Hocus Focus and Hocus Focus Analytics ◆ 111

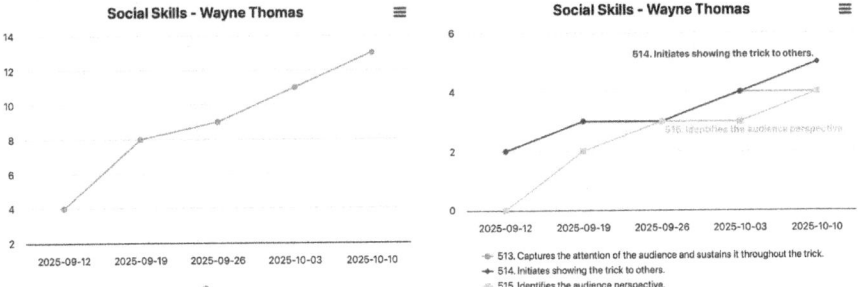

FIGURE 9.2 Sample Hocus Focus Analytics charts.

self-esteem. It allows students to see that success can be achieved through hard work and attention to task.

These are the words of one special educator who incorporated the HFSC in her classroom:

> My students blew me away! I feel that my paraprofessional and I have very high expectations for our students, but we were a bit concerned about how they would respond to Kevin's visit. We didn't know how well our students would do following multi-step directions, or if they would ask questions when lost or confused. We definitely underestimated them. They watched carefully and followed every direction. They asked each other questions and worked collaboratively to master the tricks. They respected, encouraged, and praised one another throughout the process. They were incredible!
>
> I expected improvement in their confidence, but wasn't prepared for the level of confidence that came about as a result of Hocus Focus®. They realized that they were doing things that most adults (including myself) would have trouble with! The climate in my classroom changed as well because this program required them to interact among themselves and encourage one another.
>
> Every child deserves to feel the confidence and success that comes from applying Kevin's methods. Seeing the excitement in their classroom firsthand would remind any teacher why they chose this profession in the first place. What Kevin's program does for education is truly magical!

Summary

The *Hocus Focus Supplemental Curriculum* (HFSC) is a research-based, arts-integrated program that uses magic tricks to support student growth across five developmental areas: cognition, creativity, communication, motor skills, and social skills.

Grounded in theories of multiple intelligences and experiential learning, HFSC is designed to engage students through modeling, coaching, and performance-based activities. Magic tricks provide a unique platform for storytelling, problem-solving, coordination, and expression. To assess student progress, researchers developed the *Hocus Focus Analytics* (HFA) tool—a 15-item, highly reliable scale designed for ease of use in the classroom. Teachers can track student growth in key areas that are often difficult to measure through traditional assessments. This tool empowers educators to document meaningful progress, advocate for arts-based instruction, and tailor lessons to diverse learning needs. The HFSC and HFA together offer an innovative, engaging, and inclusive approach to supporting student success in any classroom setting.

References

Anderson, A., & Berry, K. (2017). Tableau's influence on the oral language skills of students with language-based learning disabilities. *Learning Disabilities: A Multidisciplinary Journal, 22*(1), 1–20.

Duffy, B., & Fuller, R. (2010). Role of music therapy in social skills development in children with moderate intellectual disability. *Journal of Applied Research in Intellectual Disabilities, 13*(2), 77–89. https://doi.org/10.1046/j.1468-3148.2000.00011.x

Eisner, E. (2002). *The Arts and the creation of mind.* Yale University Press.

Ezell, D., & Klein-Ezell, C. E. (2003). M.A.G.I.C. W.O.R.K.S (Motivating activities geared-to instilling confidence—wonderful opportunities to raise kid's self-esteem). *Education and Training in Developmental Disabilities, 38*(4), 441–450.

Frith, G. H., & Walker, J. C. (1983). Magic as motivation for handicapped students. *Teaching Exceptional Children, 15*(2), 108–110.

Gardner, H. (1993). *Multiple intelligences: The theory in practice.* New York: Basic Books Inc.

Gerber, B., & Horoschak, L. (2012). An attack on the Tower of Babel: Creating a National Arts/Special Education Resource Center. In *Proceedings from the Kennedy Center's Intersection of Arts Education and Special Education: Exemplary Programs and Approaches*, Washington, DC (pp. 113–125).

Hines, A., Bundy, A. C., Black, D., Haertsch, M., & Wallen, M. (2019). Upper limb function of children with unilateral cerebral palsy after a magic-themed HABIT: A pre-post- study with 3- and 6-month follow-up. *Physical & Occupational Therapy in Pediatrics, 39*(4), 404–419. https://doi.org/10.1080/01942638.2018.1505802

Hines, A., Bundy, A. C., Haertsch, M., & Wallen, M. (2018). A magic-themed upper limb intervention for children with unilateral cerebral palsy: The perspectives of parents. *Developmental Neurorehabilitation, 22*, 104–110. https://doi.org/10.1080/17518423.2018.1442372

Kaufman, S. B. (2017). Curiosity is a unique market of academic success. *The Atlantic*, July 24, 2017.

MacLean, J. (2008). The art of inclusion. *Canadian Review of Art Education, 35*, 75–97.

O'Rourke, S., Spencer, K., & Kelly, F. (2018). Development and psychometric investigation of an arts integrated assessment instrument for educators. *Journal for Learning Through the Arts, 14*(1), 1–20. https://escholarship.org/uc/item/0mx5z5xd, https://doi.org/10.21977/D914137309

Posner, M., Rothbart, M., Sheese, B., & Kieras, J. (2008). How arts training influences cognition. In C. Asbury & B. Rich (Eds.), *Learning, arts, and the brain: The Dana Consortium report on arts and cognition* (pp. 1–10). Dana Press.

Ruppert, S. (2006). Critical evidence - how the arts benefit student achievement. Arts Education in Maryland Schools Alliance report. https://files.eric.ed.gov/fulltext/ED529766.pdf

Spencer, K. (2012). Hocus Focus: Evaluating the academic and functional benefits of integrating magic tricks in the classroom. *The Journal of the International Association of Special Education, 13*(1), 87–99. https://www.researchgate.net/publication/288989190_Hocus_Focus_Evaluating_the_Academic_and_Functional_Benefits_of_Integrating_Magic_Tricks_in_the_Classroom

Spencer, K., & Balmer, S. (2020, February). A pilot study: Magic tricks in the ELL classroom increasing verbal communication initiative and self-efficacy. *English Language Teaching and Linguistics Studies, 2*(1), 11–26. https://doi.org/10.22158/eltls.v2n1p11

Spencer, K., Yuen, H., Jenkins, G., Kirklin, K., Griffin, A., Vogtle, L., & Davis, D. (2020, March). Evaluation of a magic camp for children with hemiparesis: A pilot study. *Occupational Therapy in Health Care, 34*(2), 155–170. https://doi.org/10.1080/07380577.2020.1741055

Yazici, E. (2017, May). The impact of art education program on the social skills of preschool children. *Journal of Education and Training Studies*, *5*(5), 17–26.

Yuen, H., Spencer, K., Kirklin, K., Edwards, L., & Jenkins, G. (2021). Contribution of a virtual magic camp to enhancing self-esteem in children with ADHD: A pilot study. *Health Psychology Research*, *9*(1), 26986. https://doi.org/10.52965/001c.26986

Yuen, H., Spencer, K., Kirklin, K., Edwards, L., & Jenkins, G. (2023). Virtual magic camp to improve social skills and self-esteem in children with autism: A pilot study. *American Journal of Occupational Therapy*, *77*(1), 7701205120.

10

The Final Bow

In every performance I've given on stage, there came a moment when it was time to take my final bow. It was not the moment the magic ended. It was the moment where I acknowledged the wonder that had unfolded and the people who made it all possible. I've felt that bow in theaters, under stage lights. But, more recently, I've felt it in classrooms, surrounded by students whose courage and creativity surpass any illusion I could have ever performed. In teaching—especially in the sacred space of special education—this final bow becomes something deeper. It is a recognition of something far greater than ourselves. It is a bow to the resilience of our students, to the imagination that carried us through challenges, and to the enduring promise that there is always more magic to come.

While this book has explored the world of teaching and learning broadly, through classrooms of all kinds and students of every ability, I want to share something personal here at the end: my work, heart, and passion have always been rooted in special education. The amazing students I've worked with—each with their own ways of thinking, moving, communicating, and connecting—have shaped every idea in this book. They've taught me what real magic looks like.

But this is not a chapter for special educators alone. Whether you teach in a general education setting or a specialized program and whether you work in a therapy room or a bustling classroom, the magic we've explored together belongs to you, too. Because

DOI: 10.4324/9781003659914-12

every student deserves wonder. Every learner benefits from imagination, creativity, and connection. And every teacher—no matter the setting—has the power to create transformative experiences.

Throughout this book, we've walked the path of the *MAGICIAN*: Motivation, Active learning, Goal-directed instruction, Imagination, Creativity and curiosity, Immersion, Affirmation, and Natural rapport. Each chapter offered a lens through which we can reimagine our roles as educators, guides, and, yes, even artists in the classroom.

But now, as we close this curtain, let's direct our spotlight toward the place where magic matters most: the world of special education.

Teaching Where the Magic Is Needed Most

Special education is not a footnote in the story of teaching. It is the proving ground of everything we claim to believe about learning, equity, and the power of the human spirit. It's easy to perform dazzling tricks for audiences who already believe. It's far more meaningful to offer wonder, joy, and transformation in places that have been overlooked, underestimated, or misunderstood.

In the special education classroom, the magician's role becomes deeply intentional. Here, student motivation isn't assumed—it must be sparked. Active learning must be shaped

FIGURE 10.1 Dr. Kevin Spencer teaches a magic trick to an elementary school boy. Photo by Aiken Performing Arts (SC).

around sensory, emotional, and cognitive differences. Goals aren't abstract—they're hard-won milestones. Imagination, creativity, immersion, affirmation, rapport: these are not luxuries—they're lifelines.

The Quiet Magic

Magic in special education is rarely loud. It's not the grand illusion or the standing ovation. It's a whispered word from a nonverbal child. It's a flicker of eye contact. A hand raised. A sudden burst of laughter from someone who never laughs in groups. It's a child using both hands to complete a task after weeks of effort. It's a student recalling yesterday's lesson—not just with accuracy, but with pride.

These are the miracles that don't make headlines. But they're the heart of what we do.

To teach like a magician in special education is to become fluent in small wonders. To craft lessons like routines, knowing that timing, surprise, and emotional resonance matter just as much as content. It's to understand that your audience may not always applaud, but they're watching. Feeling. Absorbing. And sometimes, they are transforming.

A Different Kind of Sleight of Hand

Magicians are masters of attention, perception, awareness, and belief. Educators must be too and special educators even more so. We shift focus from what a child *can't* do to what they *might* do. We control the frame—not to deceive, but to uplift. We guide the gaze of the classroom, helping every student feel seen and capable. We perform "sleights of hand" that look like ordinary teaching but carry extraordinary purpose. A sensory bin becomes a language lab. A movement break becomes a regulation ritual. A puppet show becomes a social story. A game becomes a diagnostic tool. We blend art and science, intention and intuition.

We plan obsessively and improvise constantly. We disappear behind the scenes so our students can shine. That's magic.

You Are the Trick

If there's one lesson that threads through this entire book, it's this: the magic isn't in the trick. It's in the magician. In special education, this is doubly true. The tools, techniques, and frameworks we use matter—but they're all animated by who *you* are: your joy, your patience, your presence, your refusal to give up. Your willingness to try again. Your capacity to celebrate what others ignore. Your deep belief that every child has worth—and potential. You are the most powerful part of the lesson plan. Not because you're flawless, but because you care deeply and create bravely. That's what students remember. That's what changes lives.

A Framework Revisited—Through the Lens of Special Education

Let's take one last look at the MAGICIAN framework, this time through the eyes of a special educator.

- **M is for Motivation**: Here, we find intrinsic drive not by dangling rewards but by lighting sparks. Motivation is cultivated through trust, surprise, joy, and success—even in tiny doses.
- **A is for Active Learning**: Our students learn by doing, by moving, and by engaging all their senses. Worksheets won't reach them. Experiences will.
- **G is for Goal-Directed Instruction**: IEPs may guide our path, but the real magic is in aligning learning targets with the child's story, their interests, and their emerging voice.
- **I is for Imaginative Teaching**: The imaginative classroom is a sanctuary. It allows students to explore identity, test reality, and expand what they believe is possible.

- **C is for Creativity and Curiosity**: In special education, creativity isn't an add-on—it's essential. When traditional methods fall short, we invent new ones. We stay curious about what *might* work.
- **I is for Immersion**: Learning must be felt, not just taught. When we are fully immersed in our classrooms, we create access points for every learner.
- **A is for Affirmation**: Our words matter. We affirm more than correct. We notice effort. We name progress. We see strengths before deficits.
- **N is for Natural Rapport**: Relationship is the foundation. Before curriculum, before content, there is connection. Students know when they are liked. That knowing opens every door.

This isn't a theoretical model—it's a living practice. It's been shaped by real students, real struggles, and real magic.

To Those Who Stay after the Show

If you are reading this final chapter, you are someone who stays after the curtain falls. You are someone who believes there is more to discover, more to give, and more to become. You are someone who is willing to make magic—not for fame or applause, but because you know that education, at its best, is sacred.

You are not alone. There is a growing chorus of educators, therapists, artists, and advocates who are reimagining what's possible. Who believe that wonder belongs in every classroom. Who are rewriting the story of what it means to teach—and to reach—every child.

Let us take our final bow together—not as a farewell, but as a promise. A promise to keep creating. To keep connecting. To keep choosing magic when it would be easier to settle for the mundane. Thank you for indulging my thinking, my stories, and this philosophy of teaching that embraces wonder, risk, and deep human connection. Writing this book has been a way to share not only ideas, but a belief—that teaching is both an art and a calling and that each of us has the capacity to make it magical. I'm grateful that you've walked this path with me, open to the possibility that being the best teacher we can be means leading with heart, imagination, and the courage to believe in every child's potential.

Because in the end, teaching like a magician isn't about tricks. It's about transformation. And the world needs more of that.

For Product Safety Concerns and Information please contact our EU representative GPSR@taylorandfrancis.com
Taylor & Francis Verlag GmbH, Kaufingerstraße 24, 80331 München, Germany

www.ingramcontent.com/pod-product-compliance
Lightning Source LLC
Chambersburg PA
CBHW070403240426
43661CB00056B/2524